This book is dedicated
to Walter Griem, one of the
founders of the
"Aquarium Hamburg" company

© 1983
Tetra Press
D-4520 Melle 1, P.O.Box 1580, West Germany
All rights reserved, incl. film, broadcasting, television as well as the reprinting.
Translation: C. Rasmussen
1st edition 1976 in West Germany
Printed in West Germany
Cover Photo: Oranda

Professor W. Ladiges

Cold-Water Fish in the Home and Garden

Introduction

One encouraging aspect of the present "wave of nostalgia" is the return to more unusual hobbies. This covers the newly awakened interest in native European and North American cold-water fish as well as in the many different types of goldfish. Recently, an Englishman described this fact as "a revival of the origins of the aquatic hobby".

Although the fish described in this book do not require a heated tank, the term "cold-water fish" is not quite correct, as most of the time these species will not tolerate temperatures below 7 or 8°C (45°F). Fish mentioned in this book can be easily maintained at a normal room temperature with its slight seasonal changes. Apart from a few exceptions this is true for the pond fish mentioned in this booklet too.

Other points that might be important have been collated in this little book: the reader will find useful information about his pets, since cold-water fish are not without problems!

I would like to thank Gerhard Brünner for his contribution "Plants in Cold-Water Tanks and Garden Ponds" as well as for the photographs. The Care and Feeding Table for the fish mentioned in this book has been compiled by Hans A. Baensch. I wish to express my special thanks to him for his endeavours regarding this book.

PROF. DR. W. LADIGES

Contents

Bitterling make an ideal aquarium fish and have fascinating spawning habits. Their eggs are laid in freshwater mussels, and this fish cannot breed in their absence.

Principles
of Cold-Water Fish Keeping

The large number of tropical fish offered on the market today has one advantage: nearly all of them seem to be more suitable as pets than the majority of cold-water fish. Apart from a few species, cold-water fish grow relatively rapidly and their final size is quite considerable. Although they do not require any extra heating in their tank, their other demands are by no means lower than those of tropical fish. On the contrary: cold-water fish are often more demanding and require more attention. Nevertheless, to watch them and to keep them successfully may be more exciting. The hobbyist who loves his native land will often find a lot of pleasure when maintaining fish from local ponds and streams.

There are only a few species mentioned in this book: these, however, are comparatively easy to obtain. However the deplorable condition of many streams and rivers means that in some areas there remain no fish at all. Waters that contain fish are often either private or commercially used for the breeding of fish. In both cases the hobbyist is not allowed to collect his pets there. Only the aquarist who is in touch with the local laws may have the chance to collect his own specimens. Hobbyists, who can afford it, visit tropical countries nowadays in order to catch their own fish there. Favourable travelling conditions and special hobbyist travel groups make this possible.

Both U.S. and metric units have been used in this book.
To convert litres to U.S. gallons multiply by 0.264.
To convert °C to °F multiply by 1.8 and add 32.
To convert centimetres (cm) to inches (ins) multiply by 0.39.

The Cold-Water Tank

Selecting the Container, the Site, and the Fish

The tank for cold-water fish does not differ from the aquarium for tropical fish with regard to technical equipment and construction. Silicone sealed glass tanks as well as plastic (acrylic) tanks are suitable. The aquarist should be careful with plastic tanks as they are easily scratched.

The aquarium size is of great importance. Most cold-water species become substantially larger than tropical fish and most of the time cold-water fish are active swimmers, requiring plenty of free swimming space. Accordingly, the tank should be at least 1 m (3 feet) long, preferably larger.

It is easy to calculate the capacity of the tank:
the hobbyist has to multiply length by height by width (all in centimetres) and divide by 1000. The resulting figure is tank capacity in litres. To convert litres to U.S. gallons multiply by 0.264.

However, the aquarist has to pay attention to the fact that the glass sides, the bottom material, as well as the stones, will affect the amount of water in the tank. It is important for the life of your fish to find out the exact capacity of your tank. This is especially true for the addition of chemical preparations.

Example:
Length of the tank   80 cm
Height   40 cm
Width   30 cm
80 x 30 x 40 = 96,000 ÷ 1,000 = 96
Accordingly the tank capacity is 96 litres (25 U.S. gallons).

10 % should be deducted from this figure to allow for bottom material and decorations which would leave 85 litres.

The height of a tank is important only when American sunfish are kept, as they will appear at their best in tanks more than 40 cm (16 inches) high. Otherwise, height and depth may vary according to the individual styling of the tank.

If the hobbyist for example wants to recreate a little creek, the tank has to be shallower than when installing an aquarium for carp-like fish (bottom feeders!). Goldfish should preferably be kept in a tank of more than 40 cm depth. As plants for these tanks require plenty of light it is recommended to choose a bright place when selecting the site of the tank. The aquarist has to take this into consideration when installing the artificial lighting and this is referred to on page 26 of this book.

Avoid placing your aquarium above a radiator or in front of south- or west-facing windows. A rapid marked change of the water temperature has to be avoided in all circumstances. Furthermore, too much direct sunlight will encourage unsightly algae.

When selecting the fish, the following rule of thumb should be taken into consideration:
3 litres (1.5 U.S. gallons) of water for 1 cm (0.4 inch) of fish when carp-like fish are concerned,
5 litres (2.5 U.S. gallons) of water for 1 cm (0.4 inch) of fish when other fish are concerned.
These rules cannot be applied when tropical fish are kept.

The experienced hobbyist may keep more fish than this rule allows when using high quality filtration and aeration equipment. It is important, however, to bear in mind that fish grow rapidly but that the tank does not! It is advisable to remove your fish from the tank after they have attained a size of approximately 15–20 cm (about 6–7 inches). They should then be put into the garden pond or given to large, public show tanks. Another possibility is to put them back to native streams and rivers, if that is where they came from!

Technical Equipment for the Aquarium

Filtration

The installation of an effective internal and/ or external filter is important. Only a few species, as for example North-American sunfish, require additional aeration of the tank. The keeping of sticklebacks, dwarf catfish, and Koi is possible without the installation of filtration and aeration equipment, so long as the tank is not over-crowded. In these tanks, however, rich plant life is necessary. Some types of hardy goldfish can be maintained like this, too. In a tank with goldfish and other carp-like fish the aquarist has to pay attention to the water quality as these greedy feeders will pollute the water rather rapidly. Accordingly, the hobbyist often has to remove mulm and debris, and part of the water has to be renewed, quite frequently. Appropriate filtration equipment would save the hobbyist this work. The **Brillant Filter** is recommended for small tanks up to 80 cm (31 inches) in length, larger tanks require a power filter.

When using a power filter it is not necessary to install an air pump, and hence it is not possible to use an air stone. On a warm day, the temperature of an unheated tank may well reach more than 20°C (68°F) which will lower the oxygen content of the water, as warm water cannot hold as much oxygen as cool water. Your fish, however, require more oxygen because of an increased

Aquarium filters

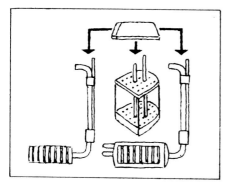

metabolism. Plastic tubing should then be used to direct the outlet of the power filter onto the water surface this creating turbulence and aiding oxygen entry into the water.

An air stone, placed approximately 5 cm above the tank bottom. Only when the water surface is moved will oxygen enter the water efficiently.

Regular cleaning of the internal and external filter is especially important in warm weather, as dirty and old filter masses can consume quite a lot of oxygen.
If fish do not have sufficient oxygen – the hobbyist may see this from an increased movement of the gills and mouth – it is important to do the following immediately:
1. Change 1/3 of the water and add **Aqua Safe**
2. Clean the filter
3. Remove mulm and dirt from the tank bottom
4. Increase the output of the filtration and/ or aeration equipment
5. Check the temperature! When exposed to direct sunlight (temperature of more than 22°C, 72°F) the tank has to be shaded for protection.

Air Pumps

When selecting the tank equipment it is recommended to choose good quality items, as the health of your fish and plants depend on them. With the help of an air pump is it possible to operate an air stone as well as a power filter. This air stone should always be placed near (but not on) the aquarium floor, in order to avoid dirt particles being stirred up. The air pump should always be installed above the level of the water so that the back-siphoning of water cannot harm it.

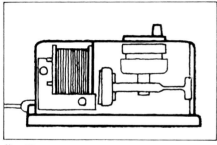
Air pump

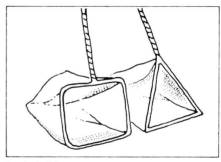
Nets for the fish

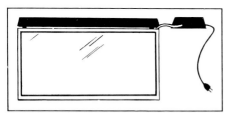
Tank with pump above the water level to prevent back siphoning

Thermometer

It is recommended to choose a reliable thermometer, for example the **Tetra Thermometer**, the only tank thermometer with a guarantee and a deviation of less than ± 1°C.

Temperature Rule

The temperature of a cold-water tank should not exceed 20°C (68°F) − goldfish will tolerate temperatures up to 22°C.

Selecting Nets

From time to time it may be necessary to remove fish from the tank and the aquarist needs at least one net. Fish nets are obtainable in different sizes, relative to the size of the tank. The easiest way to catch the fish is by using two nets: a larger one which should be kept in readiness in one corner of the tank and a smaller one being used to drive the fish into it.

For the garden pond larger long-handled nets are required. Your dealer will recommend and explain the alternatives depending on your tank size and fish.

Bottom Material

Healthy plant life depends on the quality of the bottom material. Chalk-free gravel of different sizes is obtainable from your local supplier. Fine sand or marble gravel are not suitable.

Of the materials illustrated below those above and left are most suitable; those below and on the right are not suited as they are of light color and of the wrong size.

Gravel for the aquarium (see text)

9

3. Installing the Filter and Decorations

After installing the inside or outside filter, the filter material should be inserted. With the help of an air line the filter should then be connected to the pump. After that the thermometer should be placed on one of the side glasses enabling the hobbyist to read it easily.

Some of the decorations should be used to hide the inside filter, thus improving the general appearance of the tank. Aquascape the aquarium with rocks so that they slope down towards the front.

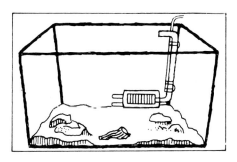

Setting Up Your Aquarium

1. The Cleaning of the Tank and the Equipment

Thoroughly wash the aquarium and the aquarium equipment and decorations with warm water. The decorations should be brushed under running tap water. To wash the gravel put it in a plastic pan or bucket and add running water. After that the gravel should be stirred until the water stays clear and is free of debris. Do not use soap or detergents.

2. Tank Bottom

When inserting the gravel, the aquarist should pay attention to the fact that it must slopes down towards the front. This will give a better appearance and help the plants at the rear by giving sufficient depth for root growth. Gravel depth should vary between 4–8 cm (about 2–3 inches).

4. Adding the Water

Fill the aquarium to approximately half its depth. Pour the water onto a plate or into the cup of your hand so it will not disturb the gravel.

If you are adding water plants now, be sure to use **AquaSafe** first. This will protect fish and plants from shock when entering their new environment.

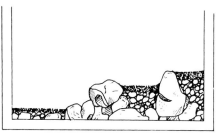

Use rocks and gravel to create an attractive aquascape

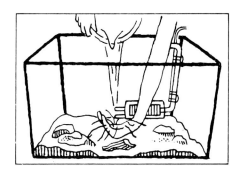

5. Plants

Foul and decaying leaves should be removed, the roots should not be longer than 3–4 cm (about 1½ inches). Plants of the same family should be placed in one group; planted singly they will not look good in the tank. Tall growing plants should be placed in the rear or at both sides of the tank, smaller species in the middle and the foreground. They should be inserted in such a way that the "neck" of the root is still to be seen. If they have a tendency to "float-up" repeatedly they should be weighted. Your dealer will assist you by explaining the various methods.

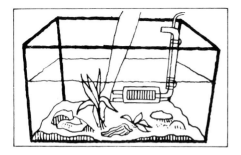

6. Topping Up

After all the plants have been inserted, the tank should be filled to near the top. There should be 2–3 cm air space left at the top of tanks. Again, pour the water in such a way that you do not disturb your aqua-scaping and gravel.

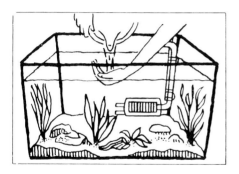

7. Starting the Filter

Plug in your air pump. If the filter does not work properly (large air bubbles, or too little water) the air outlet has to be adjusted. Before installing a power filter, carefully read the manufacturer's instructions.

8. Checking the Water Temperature

The water temperature should be checked daily. Most cold-water fish thrive best at a temperature of about 16–20°C (65°F).

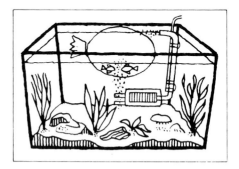

9. Adding the Fish

Usually the fish are transported in plastic bags or jars from the store. These containers should be placed into the tank for approximately 5–10 minutes. After that, small amounts of tank water should be added slowly to the container. This is very important because of the different water conditions, for example pH value and temperature. The new fish should be given some time to accustom themselves to the new aquarium water. To protect the fish from shock, **Aqua-Safe** should be added. After the water temperature in the container is the same as in the aquarium, the fish may be released into their new environment (about 20 minutes).

10. Cover the Aquarium

Place the condensation tray on top of the aquarium and install the lighting in the hood. Turn on the tank light for 10–14 hours daily, dependent on the existing daylight conditions (see page 26).

Just a few of the many varieties of the fancy goldfish.
Remarkably they are all one species – *Carassius auratus*

11. First Feeding

It is advisable not to feed your new fish until they have adapted themselves to their new surroundings. If they are hiding in corners, "standing around" or showing pale colors, it is possible that something is out of order.

> Is the temperature correct?
> Was the water poorly conditioned?
> Was **AquaSafe** added?
> Is the lighting and the color of the gravel creating too light an environment? Do the plants and rocks offer enough hiding places?
> Are the fish healthy? (Or do they show any little white spots or fungus on their fins and body?)

During the first weeks, your new fish should be fed sparingly. Remember that too much food will foul the water.
It is sufficient to feed your fish twice a day. The food should be consumed in 2–3 minutes. After 3–4 weeks – when the tank is biologically "stable" – you may start to feed your fish 3–4 times daily. By this time, useful bacteria have developed, which will neutralize the fish's metabolic waste products.

If you want to watch your fish while feeding them it is best to feed them in small amounts.

> It is recommended to select the food according to the characteristics and the requirements of your fish.
> Do not feed more than is consumed in 2–3 minutes.
> Dry food should be fed in small portions only. Avoid pouring it from the drum, directly into the water.
> Watch your fish while feeding them. Try to determine their food requirements and maintain that level; this varies according to the water temperature and the season.
> Watch out that no excess food decays and pollutes the tank water.

Water Quality

The well-being and the health of your fish depend on the water quality. The species mentioned in this book do not have special requirements with regard to the tank water (with a few exceptions). In almost all instances, tap water will be fine as long as it is free from chlorine and at the correct temperature. With the help of **AquaSafe** dangerous substances in the water are destroyed and made safe for your tank.
However, the following hints may prove useful. Contrary to most tropical fish species, slightly alkaline water is more favourable than slightly acid or neutral water for the species described in this book. However, attention should be paid to the water hardness. Very hard water is dangerous to most long-finned goldfish varieties.

> $1/3$ of the water of your tank has to be changed every 2–3 weeks.
> Do not forget to add **AquaSafe** at each water change.

The water hardness is easily measured with the **TetraTest KH Kit**. The carbonate hardness should range from 10–20°, if the readings are higher, rain water should be added. If the water is too soft, add a little bit of gypsum or limestone.

The aquarium as well as the garden pond is generally best at a value of pH 7 to pH 8. Water below pH 7 is called "acid", water above pH 7 "alkaline". The pH value is easily determined with the **TetraTest pH I** (range pH 1 – pH 7.5) and the **TetraTest pH II** (starting at pH 7.5). By measuring the pH value of your tank, you can easily see whether for instance the bottom materials are suitable or not. Gravel with a high chalk content will increase the water hardness and the tank water may become very alkaline.

> Before releasing your fish into your new garden pond, check whether the pH value is below 8.
> If not, it is absolutely necessary to check that any new concrete or an algal bloom are not adverely affecting the pH. Your water garden specialist dealer will advise on this.

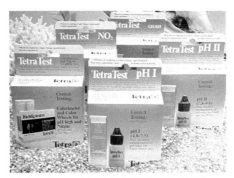

Tetra test kits accurately measure water quality – simply!

Two Suggestions for a Natural Tank Set-up

In this section I would like to make two suggestions for the styling of a cold-water tank. The decoration is not too expensive and many of the species mentioned in this book can be easily maintained in an environment as described below:

1. Quite a number of fish species – especially carp-like fish and goldfish – like to dig the tank bottom in search of live food, larvae or other leftovers. In such a tank, plants are not easy to grow, as the fish uproot them. My suggestion to solve this problem has the advantage that it might be used for other fish not mentioned in this book.

The tank (not less than 1 m or 3 feet in length) is divided lengthwise into two halves by a wooden board (petrified wood, drift wood that has been soaked in fresh water for a long period of time). This wooden board is carefully fastened in the tank bottom (use a concrete/gravel mixture 1 : 3, or fibreglass) and should then be left to stand for at least two weeks if concrete has been used. It is important that the wooden board does not become dry, as this will cause tension and splitting when submerged in the water. This wooden division should at least be 15–20 cm (6–8 ins) high, according to the size of the tank.

Bottom materials should then be filled into the rear part of the tank. Washed, fine grain gravel is recommended, to which small amounts of peat and clay-soil have been added.

Especially suited as plants are spring shoots of the genus *Nuphar* (water lilies), interrupted by groups of dry reeds (very decorative!) or single groups of *Vallisneria.* When showing signs of decay the reeds have to be renewed.

In order to keep your fish from uprooting this part of the tank, it is recommended to cover the bottom with large stones. The rear part might also be suitable for the installation of an inside filter.

The front part should be filled with very fine gravel (3–8 cm deep) that has been carefully washed before, and should remain free from plants, stones or other aquascaping material, as in this part of the tank the fish may dig as much as they like and try to find food items: insect larvae, *Tubifex* or dry foods. When breeding bitterlings *(Rhodeus amarus)*, the same method of aqua-styling should be used, as their eggs are usually placed within a living mussel which buries itself and wanders in the fine gravel of the front part of the tank, where the hobbyist can easily watch them. This method may also be used where small predatory fish are concerned; the fine gravel, however, should then be substituted by large, rounded pebbles. Plant thickets of

Elodea and *Myriophyllum* are recommended; reeds should not be used or placed closely to the glass in order to avoid the fish become squashed.

2. Imagine a mossy creek, running freely between high trees: this is approximately my idea for the second suggestion, a banked tank.

I had a special tank built, where the iron frame was left out, as this would have destroyed the impression I wanted to create. (Especially suited for this second proposal are all glass tanks with silicone jointed sides.) The lateral as well as the rear glasses were of green cathedral glass, which had to be as thick as possible because of the iron frame that was left out.

I then collected rounded, flat pebbles of all sizes from a creek in the neighbourhood. The next step was to cement in the pebbles, sloping to the front, building caves and excavations. With a length of 1.20 m, such a tank should at least have a depth of 60 cm as the background decoration requires quite a lot of space. As in the creek, pebbles were spread all over the tank bottom. In order to fasten them, they were fixed to the ground with cement and later covered with crushed gravel (see comments above).

The flat pebbles were used as supports or foundations for plant cushions. After having been allowed to stand for two weeks (daily water change!) the tank was ready for use. Cushions of moss, growing on stones or wood, easily found in smaller creeks, were added. Stones and caves, reaching the water surface, were covered with bushy thickets of moss and other small plants of the above-mentioned biotope, even small ferns can live here. An experienced hobbyist might even be able to install a kind of spray system for these plant cushions with the help of a filter. It is important that an effective air stone is installed, as the filter outlet is not sufficient alone. The hobbyist should always bear in mind that this aquascape represents a creek with running water and that his fish should come from this biotope.

The following fish is especially suited for this kind of tank: a school of *Phoxinus phoxinus*. In the mossy area there may live one or two small terrapins as well as some toads or frogs. The hobbyist, however, has to be careful to avoid them escaping by installing suitable covers. In my creek tank two small crayfish used to live as well.

Fire bellied toad *(Bombina variegrata)* in a defensive posture

European fire salamander *(Salamandra salamandra)*

14

Maintenance and Care of Your Aquarium

The most common reasons given against the installation of an aquarium are the following: too much work and the possibility of water spillage. In reality, however, the amount of time spent on the care and maintenance of your tank is extremely low. It should be limited to a minimum because your hobby deals with a miniature, self-contained living world, which should not be disturbed too much. Excessive handling may even harm your fish and their planted surroundings.

It is recommended to regularly clean your tank every 2–3 weeks: this will not take more than half an hour and should consist of the following.

Cleaning Your Tank

1. Switch off the electrical equipment (remove the wall plug).
2. Remove algae from front and side glasses. **Tetra's Rapid Cleaner** will be of great assistance because of its double blade system.
3. Mulm and algae residues that gather on the tank bottom should be removed with the aid of a siphon tube or a vacuum-type bottom cleaner.
   The removal of this waste is extremely important. Failure to do so will lower the oxygen content of the water and accordingly, its general quality.
4. When thoroughly cleaning the aquarium, remove $2/3$ of the water (no more). Place a bucket into a larger bowl to avoid splashing of the water on the carpet!
5. Replace filter material or clean the filter cartridge under running tap water by repeated kneading.
6. Replace removed tank water with fresh tap water. To avoid damaging fish and plants, add **AquaSafe** before filling the aquarium (for each 10 litres or 2.6 U.S. gallons of water removed add 5 ml of **AquaSafe**). Always bring the new water to the correct (water) temperature with a little boiling water from a kettle.
7. Switch on aquarium filter.
8. Light fittings, cover glasses, front and lateral glasses should be cleaned now. Lime deposits on the cover glasses are easily removed with a blade type cleaner and a rag, soaked with diluted vinegar. Finally the front glasses should be cleaned with paper toweling and a glass cleaner.

Note:
If you use any medication against algae, do not add **FloraPride**, as this might promote algae growth. Algae problems may be controlled using the **Tetra** algal treatments, carefully following their instructions for use.

Mulm on the tank bottom is easily removed with the Tetra Bottom Cleaner.

⊙Tetra Hydro-Clean²⁰/4

The Aquarium Gravel Washer

- Removes dirt and debris
- Siphons 20 gallons in 4 minutes
- Easy starting siphon
- Maximizes under-gravel and power filtration
- Does not disturb decorations

No aquarium is cleaned unless it's Hydro-cleaned

No aquarium is cleaned unless it's Hydro-cleaned

15

Snails

Sooner or later the aquarist will find uninvited guests in his tank: snails. They find their way into the tank on plants or with live food. The most common of this is the slim American pond snail. It has a high rate of reproduction and will even attack plants.

Snails do not necessarily clean up the tank as often assumed. In fact it is almost useless to employ snails in cleaning the tank or the glass.

The Red Ramshorn Snail may also be introduced to your tank on plants. This pretty snail is harmless as long as only a few exist. If the tank is overfed they, too, will multiply and attack your plants.

Removing snails from a tank is quite simple. Switch off the light, preferably in the evening. Place an upturned saucer into the tank and put 3–5 **TabiMin** tablets on it. During the next 1–2 hours, the snails will gather around the tablets. After having switched on the light, all you need do is remove the saucer.

Snails will also invade your garden pond. Avoid the use of chemicals; these large snail species should rather be removed by hand from time to time.

the lighting there. Only by controlling the amounts of food may the hobbyist eliminate algal growth in his pond. Excessive amounts of uneaten fish food on the pond bottom and its sides should be avoided. Siting a new pond where it receives some shade from the mid-day sun, and ensuring plenty of aquatic plants are present, will also help to control algae.

For a very short time, a green clouding of the garden pool will appear in spring or summer, which is caused by masses of floating algae, for example after the introduction of water lilies.

To recommend *Lemna minor* to keep your garden pond free of algae might mean a change for the worse. Under optimal conditions – which is the case in water with plenty of plant nutrients – *Lemna minor* spreads so rapidly that after a short period of time no water surface is left free of it. If *Lemna minor* gets beyond control, it has to be removed regularly with a net. Be careful that none remain, even between other species growing at the bankside, as they will reproduce again and soon cover the water surface. Other floating plants, *Hydrocharis morsusranae* for example, are easily controlled.

Algae

Aquarium algae may become a problem; if the growth becomes to profuse, it will help to change or reduce the lighting or to use chemicals (**Tetra** algal treatments). The situation in your garden pond may become more difficult, as it is impossible to regulate

Note: not all the products mentioned in this book are available on a worldwide basis. If in doubt, consult your **Tetra** stockist.

The Garden Pond

Construction and Styling

The small garden pond – already well-known in England for a long period of time – is now appearing in the U.S.A. In Japan, "water gardens" have been around for thousands of years and are now part of the culture of that country.

Pools of no more than 6 m or 19 feet in length are called "small". There are several books with more or less detailed construction suggestions. These "do-it-yourself" instructions, however, can turn out to be tricky. Again, your dealer can assist you by explaining the various types and methods. It is advisable to buy one of these little books in order to plan the work or supervise the workman! In this book, the author would merely like to point to existing possibilities and to give some hints for the construction of your own garden pool.

1. The most simple way is by using containers already at hand, these including barrels of all kinds, concrete rings, and plastic tubs. Several of them, placed one beside the other, may look very attractive. These containers have to be carefully cleaned and washed before they are paint-

18

ed with non-toxic lining materials. Your dealer can help you by explaining the newest products on the market. These containers should not be merely let down into the earth: they have to be surrounded by a drainage layer of coarse gravel, coke, and/or clinkers so that excess rain water may seep away.

A soakaway connected to the pool bottom is absolutely essential, no matter what kind of pool is concerned. When installing the soakaway, the hobbyist has to bear in mind that it will have to be cleaned of mud and dirt. Therefore, easy access is very important.

2. Ready-made pools, and many different kinds are on the market, are very useful. They consist of hard plastic or fibreglass and are quite inexpensive. They are approximately 3 m long, but unfortunately most of them are not really deep enough. Most of these products come from the British Isles; during recent years, the Netherlands have been offering building-sets for garden pools, too. Their measurements are about 2.30 m x 1.50 m, depth 80 cm; they are quite reasonably priced. Recommended and also very suitable are childrens bathing tubs, so long as the have a sufficient depth and are rigid and robust.

Small, formal or large and informal, the possibilities when planning a garden pool are limitless.

19

The siting of ready-made pools into the individual garden landscape depends on the hobbyist. If he wants to give his pool a natural appearance, special attention has to be paid to the edges. Herbaceous plants and bushes, with aquatic marginal plants in baskets, will do wonders.

3. The building of cement or concrete pools requires careful treatment of the foundations: stones and gravel have to be removed, the earth has to be stamped down in order to make it level. The concrete can be "proofed" with products from water garden specialists. It is recommended to use screen wire for reinforcement. The wall thickness should not exceed 30 cm. When styling your concrete pool, do avoid many small bays. A single, rectangular form will do best.

For all pools, the construction of plant shelves around the edge for the marginal plants is highly recommended.

4. In spite of their artificial appearance pools of bricks and clinker look beautiful.

5. Pools made of silicone jointed, proofed roof paper turn out to be rather sturdy, when constructed carefully. Avoid stabbing the material with a sharp tool.

Another dangerous point is the possibility of injuring the liner by plant roots. In such pools, the plants should be inserted into special plant containers (baskets). The upper brim of the pond should be protected by slabs so that no animals (for instance birds) can do any harm.

6. Pools of natural materials such as clay are difficult to obtain nowadays. The raw material has to be of an excellent quality and up to 25 cm (or 10 ins.) thick. It is important to prepare the building material so that it is easy to handle but not of a fluid consistancy.

7. When styling a pool with the help of modern plastic sheeting, it is advisable to

Common pond snail *(Lymnaea stagnalis)* left
and the ramshorn snail *(Planorbis corneus)*

remove his fish from the pool in October/
November if there is any doubt about the
suitability of the pond for the overwintering
of fish.

Plants in a garden pond must be planted in a suitable depth of
water. This partially drained pond shows the shallow water
marginals around the edge and the deeper water plants in the
middle.

discuss this with the local water garden
specialist, as the qualities are being im-
proved all the time. The hobbyist should
always bear in mind that the life span of the
pool will be determined by the strength
(thickness) of the sheeting used.

8. The building of a natural ground water
pool should be restricted to the experienced
hobbyist only.

From the above-mentioned, the hobbyist
may see how many possibilities exist at
just about any price level. In any case detailed books on pool construction should be
studied carefully. When planning the pro-
ject, the hobbyist should bear in mind the
beauty of Japanese garden pools.

The newcomer to the hobby must neither
choose a pool too big nor too deep. The
exact depth of a frostproof garden pool
cannot be given as too many local facts
will set the standards. Depths of 60–100 cm
(24–40 ins.) may be regarded as frost-
resistant, depending upon local climatic
conditions. Such a pool, however, means
a constant danger for small children. Some
hobbyists should therefore be prepared to

The Hibernation of Pool Fish

For the simple, trouble-free overwintering of pool fish outside of the garden pool, a frost-free, unheated room with a stable temperature around 5–10°C (40–50°F) is required. A cellar is often an excellent location. In a warm cellar, the window may be left open. When the outside temperature is below −5°C (23°F), however, the window has to be closed.

The container for the fish should be large and offer sufficient space. At least 2 litres of water for 1 cm of fish are required. If the temperature is higher than 12°C (or 54°F), fish should be fed very sparingly. Every 6 weeks, 2/3 of the water has to be changed. A strong air pump, 2 metres of air tube, and an air stone should ensure the oxygen supply. Filter equipment is only necessary when the fish are fed, as their excrement have to be filtered out. **AquaSafe** has to be added to safely condition fresh tap water added to the container. Avoid temperature shock too.

A large tank or a plastic bath tub will do as a "hibernating container" during the winter. A concrete basin, insulated with an non-poisonous paint, is also very practical. Otherwise the basin will have to be watered for some weeks to condition the concrete! After that, the hobbyist has to check the pH value which should be below 8. Zinc baths are dangerous as they are poisonous to fish! An old enamel bath tub on the other hand is well-suited. In any case, the container used should incorporate a waste outlet in the bottom. If this is not the case, the water change has to be done with the help of a siphon tube. A waste outlet is of great advantage to get rid of the waste water. If such a water outlet cannot be installed, the hobbyist may have to use buckets for the removal of the water.

If no water change is effected, fish may be attacked by diseases, especially fungus or external parasites. In such a case, **AquaSafe** and **GeneralTonic** have to be added immediately. Only when feeding your fish should the lighting be switched on, and then only for a period of one hour (1/2 hour before and 1/2 hour after the feeding has been carried out).

If deeper than 1 m or in a mild climate, pools will hardly freeze over to an ice depth of more than 5 cm (2 ins.) in such cases it is not necessary to remove the fish.

In fall the hobbyist should remove as much vegetation from his pool as possible. In order to be able to do so, the pool water has to be removed nearly completely. Any remaining leaves will cause fermentation and under this fouling process fish will die due to the lack of oxygen and the build-up of toxic waste.

The winter ice layer will not allow an adequate oxygen supply. In order to make sure that at least a little oxygen will enter the water, bundles of straw should be stood in a large pool, which will ensure a sufficient oxygen supply. Be sure to wire the bundle tightly together.

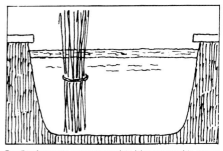

Bundle of straw to prevent complete icing over and to ensure adequate gas exchange.

If the use of a power point is available to the aquarist, he may install an air pump. This pump should be protected against rain and snow and be fastened to a wooden pile, covered with a plastic bag. This plastic bag may be tied up from below, but at the same time, the hobbyist should make sure that sufficient air may enter the pump intake. Keeping the water circulating will help prevent freezing.

Probably the best way, however to prevent complete icing over, is to install a small pool heater. These do not raise the water temperature too much − but they do keep a patch of water free from ice. They are also quite cheap to run.

In spring – by the end of March – the first sun rays will warm up the pond water and the straw can be removed or the fish transferred back into the pool. This, however, refers to healthy specimens only. By the end of May, the water frequently turns green in a few days. This will not harm the fish, but they are hardly to be seen. This clouding is due to the existence of millions of tiny algae. They disappear just as suddenly as they have come if there are no further food substances in the pool. If, however, the pool is over-fertilized (too much food) or overcrowded, the algal bloom will remain for the entire summer. Do not use remedies for combating algae as recommended for swimming pools. Minimum doses are dangerous to plant and fish life! Effective remedies to combat algae in your garden pond are available from pet shops.

Note the green algal colouration in this pond

Uninvited Guests and Parasites in the Garden Pond

A water surface, even if it is very small, attracts all kinds of aquatic animals. They may arrive during a nightly search for a new living area or just moving around, at for example spawning times. Frogs, toads, and newts are only very seldom to be found. Among the newts, *Triturus vulgaris* can most frequently be seen in the early spring at spawning time. Eggs are deposited singly in plant thickets. After a few weeks, it leaves the pond, unseen, as it came.

Other species of the family are rarely observed. *Titurus alpestris* is, however, a common inhabitant in hilly European areas. Contrary to *T. vulgaris*, this species seems to have special requirements as to its spawning environment.

Less numerous than in former times, the wellknown common frog *(Rana temporaria)* will appear in early spring. The hobbyist should let him have access to a protected area of the garden pool; too many eggs should, however, be removed into a river or other local pond.

From time to time, a spawning pair of toads *(Bufo bufo)* may visit the garden pool during this time of the year. We have to protect these nocturnal little helpers, as they feed upon destructive garden insects. It may even happen that an edible frog *(Rana esculenta)* sits at the pool's edge in full sun light. These individualists spend a roving life and do not stay longer than some few months in the summer. They are just guests and never stay; if they do, it will only be in very large pools. All these rare little animals do no harm, and any hobbyist should welcome them as guests. Similar species of amphibians also occur in North America.

Invading water insects, however, may be dangerous. Among them there are perilous robbers. First of all, *Dytiscus marginalis* should be mentioned. When fully-grown, this beetle may attain more than 5 cm (2 ins.) in length. Even in city areas it invades the garden pool. As soon as one has been seen, it is absolutely essential to catch it with a net and to remove it, as it feeds on young fish and even attacks larger specimens. *D. marginalis* deposits its eggs in the pond too and its greedy larvae are even more unpleasant.

A rare and very peaceful guest is *Hydrous piceus,* a large black, plant-eating beetle. Although it is very rare nowadays, I found a specimen some years ago in the middle of the city, which probably took the mirror-like appearance of a newly resurfaced street for water.

Water beetles of the genus *Enhydrus* are harmless and may be treated as guests. Apart from beetles, there are water bugs,

as for example *Notonecta glauca, Naucoris cimicoides,* and *Nepa rubra.* But only *Notonecta glauca* with its sucking spine may harm your fish. It will hardly be possible to catch these water bugs and to remove them; such a manoeuvre will probably disturb your fish and plants quite considerably.

Gerris species, sliding on the water surface, are harmless. They feed on dead as well as living insects.

Dragon flies of different colors, sizes, and species are a pleasant sight when visiting the garden pool. Their elegancy and their brilliant colors make them interesting to watch depositing their eggs in the water. Their predatory larvae which live in the water are not really harmful to fish. The same is also true for the numerous species of flies and their larvae.

Unfortunately the times are gone when king fishers and herons visited the garden pond. The beautiful king fisher might turn out to be dangerous to tiny fish, which we should allow him as a prize for his beauty. The heron on the other hand might empty a little pool very rapidly.

Nevertheless, no hobbyist should kill it because of its feeding habits. A very clever, witty method exists and is practicized by some English pool owners. The heron is an outsider and an individualist, avoiding other

Common European frog *(Rana temporaria)*

Common toad *(Bufo bufo)*

Edible frog *(Rana esculenta)*

Common newt *(Triturus vulgaris)*

All these amphibians are harmless in the pond and should be encouraged individuals of his species. The hobbyist should therefore buy a plastic stork, paint it as grey as a heron and place it at the pond edge.

In large cities, cats may occasionally come and try to catch fish. They do not harm fish or plant life, whereas voles and rats might become a problem because of their digging and burrowing. They even might eat away the plastic sheeting. The hobbyist should watch them carefully and eliminate them immediately if possible.

If wild ducks should visit the pond it is necessary to drive them off before they become accustomed to the place as they damage plants and embankments. A welcome guest is the moorhen, which will even appear in larger cities.

To end with, the author would like to give some special advice:

The hobbyist who wants to brighten up the grass around his pool should keep a pair of delicate, tame cranes. In such a case, however, it is impossible to have a dog at the same time.

When combating plant bugs or other destructive insects in the garden the hobbyist has to bear in mind that there is a pond nearby. Even remedies that are harmless to other living creatures, should only be applied very carefully when fish are nearly. This is especially true of insecticides.

Rather more rare alpine newt *(Triturus alpestris)*

Notorious diving beetle *(Dytiscus marginalis)*

Lacy wings of a dragon fly

Well concealed nest of a moorhen *(Gallinula chloropus)*

25

Plants in the Cold-Water Tank and the Garden Pond

Compared to the large variety of plants for the tropical tank there are only a small number of plants which are suitable for the cold-water tank.

As compared with former times, the whole approach to cold-water fishkeeping today has completely changed. For instance, the lighting. Some years ago bright daylight was an absolute must for all tanks; the aquarist of today prefers artificial lighting as modern tanks are an integral part of the decor of a room. For some water plant species, however, this is far from ideal. Many tropical floating plants as well as many cold-water plants, demanding a great amount of light, can hardly be maintained in a modern room tank, where a constant temperature delivers growth-promoting impulses but where light intensity is limiting. This disproportion between temperature and light intensity is the real problem with the so-called "cold-water plants" and the origin of many failures.

Cold-water plants require plenty of light. No doubt, direct sunlight is most favourable, at least during summer; it has, however, the disadvantage of being uncontrollable. The light intensity of the daylight will change in the course of the day. In winter, the aquarist will obviously have to install artificial lighting. Tanks not placed next to a window should always be provided with additional artificial lighting. A tank of 40 cm (about 16 ins.) depth requires 3 fluorescent lamps of tank length, possibly combined with a special device (eg. CO_2 diffuser) to stimulate plant growth. Of course, the lighting required depends on the height of the tank, too. Most cold-water plants, however, will thrive at the above-mentioned minimum quantity of 3 fluorescent lamps, if the supply of daylight is insufficient. It is important that a long day-period is maintained during winter time (more than 12 hours), corresponding to a normal summer day. Only like this can photosynthesis and healthy plants be maintained.

Most water plants, as for instance *Callitriche,* are sensitive towards too high tem-

Iris kaempferi may be used as an aquatic plant or a bog plant. It comes in many color vareties

peratures (more than 18°C, 64°F). It is therefore often better to buy imports, which are more tolerant, as for example *Elodea densa, Lagarosiphon muscoides var. Major* from South Africa, *Myriophyllum* from North America, *Sagittaria, Vallisneria*

Eichhornia crassipes, floating water hyacinth

26

Hippurus vulgaris and its characteristic appearance

or *Ludwigia.* The genuine *Cabomba caroliniana* that has adapted itself to moderate temperatures is only very rarely obtainable on the market as a pure strain. The above-mentioned species have adapted themselves better to tank life than many of the European cold-water plants.

Cold-water plants take to a variety of water conditions, as they easily adapt themselves. Plants, however, such as the freshwater moss, *Fontinalis,* growing in rapid streams, can only take the carbon dioxide they require from the free soluble carbon dioxide in the water. If this gas is exhausted, the plant will refuse to grow until fresh tap water has been added.

The hobbyist who wants to avoid a frequent water change should install a carbon dioxide (CO_2) diffuser. Some water plants are able to break down bi-carbonates. The result of this process, however, will be a growth-stopping rise in the pH. A regular checking of the pH value is therefore recommended as the normal values in the native habitats of the plants should not be exceeded. A pH value of 8 is the absolute limit for the well-being of most plants.

The bottom material should consist of larger gravel, mixed with clay. For free-floating plants, as *Ceratophyllum, Utricularia vulgaris* the tank bottom is only of importance in providing nutritional substances. A regular water change ensures the supply of trace elements and helps to avoid a concentration of wastes that might be growth-inhibiting.

Even if the cultivation of water plants from temperate zones in your home tank may offer problems, the planting of a pool is very easy and will usually work well at the first attempt. With unrestricted access to sunlight, there is a rich choice of suitable plant species available to the aquarist.

Iris pseudacorus, another marginal

27

Bladderwort, *Utricularia vulgaris*

Apart from underwater plants there are numerous floating plants and marginal plants, offering many attractive possibilities. It is up to the hobbyist to make his own choice of native plants or imported species and breeding varieties.

The charming water lilies are one of the most beautiful pool plants. When buying them the hobbyist should pay attention to the following points: choose only those plants that integrate themselves with the dimensions of your pool. Avoid selecting species that will outgrow your pond! When planted in a pool that is too shallow, *Nymphaea* produces air shoots which will cover the entire water surface by the end of the summer. Ask your dealer when buying the root-stock. Different *Nymphaea* species should be grouped in plastic baskets, filled with a mixture of garden soil and clay topped off by a layer of gravel. The root-stock should be free of decomposing matter and they should not be planted too deep (the crown should just be covered by the gravel). Water lilies love sunlight and should be exposed to maximum illumination.

Even for very small pools there are many decorative, graceful water plants available to the hobbyist: *Ranunculus aquatilis, Potamogeton natans, Polygonum amphibium,* and *Nymphoides peltata.* Some exotic plants, requiring plenty of warmth are the water hyacinth *(Eichhornia crassipes)* and *Pistia stratiotes.* Both of them require shallow water, warmed up by the sun, and maximum illumination. In autumn they have to be removed to a suitable, frost-

Water soldier *(Pistia stratoides)*
a half hardy floating plant

free area. Not as demanding as the before-mentioned species but which grews well in shallow water is *Menyanthes trifoliata.* Depending on the pool size, the hobbyist may choose among many marginal or bankside plants. *Alisma plantagoaquatica* is frequently found in Europe. Other well-suited plants are *Acorus calamus* or *Butomus umbellatus,* many emmersed *Sagittaria* species, *Iris,* and *Sparganium. Hippuris vulgaris* is especially suitable for small-sized pools. *Typha minima,* a dwarf species, does not grow higher than 60 cm (24 ins.) and is therefore suited for smaller tanks, too. Larger plants, as for example *Phragmites,* should be avoided, as they grow too high and will shadow the water surface; apart from that they might cause a silting up because of their rapid growth.

Humid spots of the embankment allow the planting of *Caltha palustris* and *Myosotis palustris* as well as *Lysimachia nummularia.*

As a general rule the hobbyist should avoid too many plants, as the pool will loose its charm when nearly entirely covered by plants. However, a healthy stocking of plants will help control algal problems.

Water plantain, *Alisma plantago aquatica* – a familiar plant

Reedmace *(Typha)* is often a bullrush

29

A Choise of Plants

1. Plants for the Cold-Water Tank

Elodea (Egeria) densa is one of the best known tank plants. Compared to *Elodea canadensis, Elodea densa* grows more abundantly and adapts easily to tank life.

The native habitat of hornwort *(Cerato-phyllum)* is slow rivers or lakes. *Cerato-phyllum demersum* has the highest rate of proliferation. Under favourable light conditions, hornwort species stay in good condition even during winter time. It may be planted in thick bushes but may as well kept freefloating.

Ludwigia species as well as the before-mentioned plants of the genus *Elodea* are "typical" tank plants. Most of the time, a cross-bred strain between *L. palustris* and *L. repens* is offered on the market; the latter, coming from temperate zones of the U.S.A., is also called *"L. mulerti"*. This plant grows more slowly in cool water, but is very hardy. *Vallisneria* are so popular with most

aquarists that I need hardly mention them. When styling a cold-water tank the hobbyist should avoid selecting large tropical species of plants. He should bear in mind that the normal room temperature should not fall below the recommended minimum for a long period of time. Well-suited for tank life and of a similar constitution as *Vallisneria* are specimens of the genus *Sagittaria,* especially *Sagittaria subulata* from Northern America.

The freshwater moss, *Fontinalis antipyretica,* is one of the delicate water plants, living in creeks, sometimes together with *Ranunculus fluitans.* As long as the carbon dioxide balance is maintained freshwater moss is a hardy tank plant.

Species of the genera *Myriophyllum* develop best in cool water. Most of the time, plants from North America are offered on the European market: *Myriophyllum hippuroides* for example. This plant grows rapidly and can withstand the winter if offered additional artificial lighting.

⑤

⑥

⑦

① *Elodea densa,* a popular aquarium plant

② Hornwort *(Ceratophyllum)*

③ *Ludwigia*

④ The hardy Vallis *(Vallisneria spiralis)*

⑤ *Fontinalis antipyretica* is a moss

⑥ *Ranunculus aquatilis*

⑦ The beautiful, delicate looking *Myriophyllum* is quite hardy

31

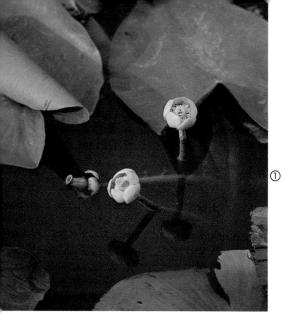

2. Plants for the Garden Pond

Water lilies should be in every garden pond; the hobbyist has to find out, however, which species will do the best in his pool, dependent on the water depth and the size of the pool. There are many breeding varieties and different species, from dwarf water lilies to real giants for large, deep pools.

The breeding variety of *Nymphaea alba,* which is even more beautiful, is called *N. marliacea albida.* However, this plant requires at least 50 cm (about 18 ins.) water depth. The same is true for *N. "Escarboucle"* with its red flowers, although this species does not grow as rapidly as the before-mentioned species.

Acorus calamus is frequently found on the banks of creeks and rivers. According to its natural environment, *Acorus calamus* should be planted near the edge of the pond. This plant is suited for smaller pools, too (maximum depth 60 cm, or about 24 ins.); it adapts itself easily and grows rapidly.

Some time ago, *Hydrocleys nymphoides* was one of the most popular aquatic plants; today it is still successfully cultivated in garden ponds. This plant requires maximum illumination if the hobbyist wants it to flower. Its native habitat are the warmer regions of North America. Therefore in autumn it has to be removed from the pond; some roots, however, should be saved and cultivated in a tank until next spring.

① to ③
No pond is really complete without a lily, although some grow quite large

④ *Acorus calamus,* a reed-like marginal

Nymphoides peltata is a rare plant nowadays, which should be protected. In spring, *N. peltata* is regularly offered on the market. The ideal plant for small ponds, as it adapts itself easily to the size of the container and the water depth. *N. peltata* has to be thinned out when growing too abundantly.

Butomus umbellatus, a coastal plant, may reach a size of nearly 1 m (40 ins.). Flowering from July to August, it easily adapts itself to any water depth. It has no special requirements and is therefore one of the most popular water plants for garden ponds.

Water irises are extremely suitable for planting on flat embankments. Japanese breeding varieties, as for example *Iris kämpferi,* have more flowers and are richer in color than *Iris pseudacorus.* Many of these colorful varieties are obtainable on the market. *I. kämpferi* is a hardy species, it should, however, be placed in dry surroundings in the winter time.

Myriophyllum brasiliense, the parrot's feather, grows upward and produces leaves above the water surface when exposed to intense light in warm water. Can withstand the winter in frostfree conditions at a temperature of approximately 10°C (30°F).

Many species of the genera *Sagittaria* are suitable for the garden pond. They have the advantage of adapting themselves easily to their new surroundings. They do not grow too high and flower regularly. Nearly all species offered on the market are hardy.

⑤ *Hydrocleys nymphoides*

⑥ *Nymphoides peltata*

⑦ *Butomus umbellata,* pink flowered

⑧ *Myriophyllum brasiliense* emerging from the pond surface

⑨ *Sagittaria,* a hardy plant

33

Cold-Water Fish

1. European Species

There are approximately 10 species of European freshwater fish suited to tank life, and they have now acquired an excellent reputation as aquarium fish. Of course, there are many other species which may be suited for tank life and a real enthusiast will even be able to breed them. For the normal aquarist, however, some of these fish become too large or they present other disadvantages. Many of the fish mentioned in this booklet are cultivated in fish farms. The following families are represented below:

Cyprinidae – seven species
Gasterosteidae – two species
Cobitidae – one species

Schneider
Alburnoides bipunctatus ①

A carp-like fish, living in schools in rapid flowing rivers. It requires lots of oxygen and should be integrated carefully to new surroundings. It accepts any kind of food, but prefers insects. Aerate tank water well.

Orfe
Leuciscus idus ②

The orfe is a carp-like fish. Native habitat: much of Europe as far as the Ural region. A very elegant variety of this species is called the golden orfe. It is white-golden in color, with red fins. The golden orfe is a very popular fish for any tank and pool as it tolerates lower temperatures. Active shoaling fish, vivid and easily visible in the garden pond. It is a greedy fish, being carnivorous but will accept dry foods as well.

Weather loach
Misgurnus fossilis ③

A cobitid fish known as the weather loach which has 10 mouth barbels, it likes quiet, shallow and warm surroundings with bushy plant thickets. It is sensitive to weather changes which is how it acquired its common name. It is otherwise quiet and nocturnal in its habits. A peaceful fish, accepting dry food, especially **TabiMin**.

34

Minnow
Phoxinus phoxinus ④

A delicate, small, active carp-like fish. Often found in the company of the trout, it is found in streams up to height of 2.000 m (6.000 feet). When first inserted into the garden pond, it requires lots of oxygen; it will, however, become easily adapted to tank life. At spawning times the males have a red belly. Phoxinus phoxinus is a shoaling fish, which feeds on small animals of all kinds, but willingly accepts dry food.

Bitterling
Rhodeus amarus ⑤

A brightly colored little carp-like fish, rather broad and flat. Its common name is the bitterling. It prefers still water with mussels (Unio) in which the spawn is deposited. The male is beautifully colored at spawning time. Will eat plant debris and small animals, but also accepts dry food.

Roach
Rutilus rutilus ⑥

The roach is one of the most common European carp-like fish. Peaceful shoaling fish, no special demands. Will not attack plants, and is easy to feed on dry food. After attaining a size of more than 10 cm (4 inches) it should be transferred to the garden pond.

Rudd
Scardinius erythrophthalmus ⑦

The rudd is a flat, carp-like white fish. It likes warm water with lots of plants. It does not require much oxygen. As Sc. erythrophthalmus prefers vegetable food, delicate water plants should be avoided. Plants of the Vallisneria genus, however, will not be touched. Most of the time, the orange-colored breeding variety has dark spots. Dry food are accepted.

⑤

⑥

⑦

35

Tench
Tinca tinca ⑧

The tench is a carp-like fish, being a bottom feeder. Requires warm water with a soft, sandy bottom. There are very pretty white and yellow-colored varieties. *Tinca tinca* is a good tank mate for all cold-water species. Peaceful, almost gluttonous will constantly stir up the bottom in search of food. Prefers plant debris etc. Accepts dry food.

Three-Spined Stickleback
Gasterosteus aculeatus ⑨

A member of the family *Gasterosteidae,* the three-spined stickleback is a small armoured fish, not very peaceful. Different species which tolerate salt water as well as freshwater forms occur. The smaller freshwater species are very well-suited for tank life, as they do not require very much oxygen. At spawning time, the brilliantly colored male builds a nest from parts of plants on the tank bottom. As it will attack other peaceful fish it should preferably be kept in a species tank. Food requirements: mainly live food. After a period of adaptation, the three-spined stickleback will accept dry food as well.

Nine-Spined Stickleback
Pungitus pungitus ⑩

Similar to the three-spined stickleback. This very delicate species inhabits small waters, such as meadow ditches. Not so popular as it has been. At spawning time the male nine-spined stickleback turns black; it builds a hanging nest in plant thickets. Feeding requirements as the above mentioned species, but more peaceful.

36

2. North American Cold-Water Fish

Apart from the above-mentioned European species, North American fish are also kept in cold-water tanks. Mostly, different species of the *Centrarchidae* family are kept. Their native habitats are the central and eastern regions of North America. Generally, they live in clear waters with a sandy bottom, singly or in shoals. Some species prefer flowing waters. Sunfish may be kept in garden ponds and in unheated tanks. They are, however, sensitive in regard to changes of water quality. When diseased and treated with chemicals they may die even more quickly. They require large tanks of at least 1 m (3 feet) in size in a bright place. Sunfish should be exposed to good illumination.

Light substrate and a rich plant life are absolutely necessary for the successful keeping of sunfish. Slow filtration and slight aeration are also recommended. When given these conditions, the sunfish will appear at their best. They spawn willingly and the parents care for the eggs and the young. After depositing their eggs in a sandy hole in the tank bottom, the male guards the eggs; this period may take three weeks, as the young fish – in addition to the eggs – are guarded as well. Often, spawning occurs only in a garden pond. As inhabitants of temperate zones, sunfish have a seasonal spawning period. Live foods of all kinds are necessary. Only young fish which have been adapted to it right from the start, will accept dry foods as well. Adult specimens accept small fish as well as lean raw meat and earthworms.

Flier
Centrarchus macropterus ①

This fish with its beautiful fins will not grow larger than 12 cm (about 5 ins.). It accepts live foods of all kinds. Unfortunately, *C. macropterus* will loose part of its striking appearance when adult.

Dwarf sunfish
Elassoma evergladei ②

Tiny, charming sunfish, is only 3.5 cm (about 1½ ins.) in size. Can withstand a variety of temperatures and water conditions. Excellently suited for small tanks. Breeds willingly. Sexes are easy to tell because of the differences in color and body shape. Parents will not attack their tiny young. The dwarf sunfish likes plant thickets where it moves in an odd manner, which looks almost like walking. Accepts dry food.

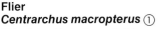

Diamond sunfish
Enneacanthus obesus ③

This small fish has special demands with regard to the water temperature and is therefore only occasionally suited for the outdoor pool. In the home tank, however, it is one of the most beautiful fish species, with its large, reddish-brown fins. Plant thickets and fine sand in which they hide are recommended. Somewhat timid and therefore preferably kept in shoals.

Sunfish of the Genus *Lepomis* ④

L. auritus, L. cyanellus, and *L. gibbosus* are the three species that most often available. *L. gibbosus* is the most beautiful of the three. It is, however, a predatory fish. According to its appearance it is called "pumkinseed". These three sunfish are ideal for the outdoor pool. After a period of adaptation they will accept lean, raw meat pieces. Our photograph shows young *L. gibbosus.*

Black-banded sunfish
Mesogonistius chaetodon ⑤

One of the smaller sunfish, which will not attain more than 10 cm (4 ins.) in size. It likes peaceful surroundings. Not suited for the community tank. Very sensitive towards nitrite. A partial change of the water is therefore recommended from time to time. **AquaSafe** should be added to the fresh tap water. Do not use soft water (less than 10° DH).

Black-banded sunfish should preferably be kept by themselves. Only live foods are accepted.

Only a few other aquarium fish come from the freshwater fauna of North America. *Fundulus* species, wellknown to the experienced hobbyist, are not mentioned in this booklet. Accordingly, there remain only two other popular species which are commonly anvitable on the market.

Brown bullhead
Ictalurus nebulosus ⑥

One of the smaller species of catfish (also known as the brown bullhead) from regions east of the Rocky Mountains. Young fish with their golden or silver shimmering "cat's eyes" and their barbels are very pretty. They like to hide in caves. Willingly accept dry foods and earth-worms. Larger specimens might attack smaller tank mates.

Eastern mudminnow
Umbra pygmaea ⑦

This fish from the lowlands of Long Island as far as the Neuse River is well-suited for tank life. American species differ from the European, which has only a one-spined dorsal fin, whereas the American has three. Peaceful fish, which likes quiet well-planted tanks. No special demands. The female guards the eggs. If necessary. *U. pygmaea* can take oxygen from the atmosphere.

3. Cold-Water Fish from Asia

White cloud mountain minnow
Tanichthys albonubes ⑧

This fish comes originally from China. It is a very popular inmate of the heated tropical tank. Will thrive better when kept in unheated tanks at room temperature, which is illustrated by its willingness to spawn. Recommended as a tank mate to small goldfish.

Zacco platypus ⑨

One of the hardy Cyprinids which has recently been imported from Japan. The male is beautifully colored and finned. A predatory glutton. Quick, active fish with no special requirements. It likes to jump. Well-suited for the outdoor pool (attains up to 18 cm in length).

Apart from *Tanichthys albonubes* and *Zacco platypus,* East-Asian enthusiasts provided us with two wild cyprinids which are a monument to the fish breeders art. They helped to make fish keeping popular, not only as a means for providing food for Man, but as a decoration and for entertainment. We are talking about the goldfish *(Carassius auratus)* with its often bizarre varieties and the "Koi", *Cyprinus carpio.* The goldfish is one of the most popular ornamental fish. In view of its importance a special chapter of this book will deal with it. The Koi plays an outstanding role in the folk life of Japan and it is on its way to conquer North America and Europe. In England it has been known as an inhabitant of the outdoor pool for sometime.

⑥

⑦

Details about the Origin and History of the Goldfish

The Goldfish or Chi-yu of Old China and Japan

In the books of the classical poets of Old China we find the first details about a golden fish, the Chi-yu. Mr. Sh. C. Chen presented all available data in a paper, first published in *Scientia Sinica* in 1956. According to his findings, the evolution and development of this fish, the youngest among our domestic animals, is as follows.

The oldest report about a golden fish dates back to the first years of the Sung-Dynasty (960–1126 a.d.). Governor Ting-Yen-tsan is said to be the first one to lay out a "goldfish pool" in Kiahsing, soon followed by others, in Hangtschou and Nanping. All these pools were situated in the neighbourhood of temples. Monks and priests shared the duties of caring for these golden fish. It was strictly forbidden to catch these fish and to eat them. Chen calls this the period of "half-domestication". It does not seem that special color variations existed at that time; merely the red color showing different grades of intensity. SuTse meh (1008–1048 a.d.) talked about shades from the "delicate pink" of the plum flower to the "meat red" of the crane head.

In these pools the so-called golden fish (or "gold fish") lived together with the wild goldfish, from which they were descended.

Just some of the many forms of the goldfish – from the fantail (top left) to the moor (bottom left) and the bubble-eye (bottom right)

40

It was not until 1163 that artificial pools were built at the court of the Chinese emperor and the estates of the nobility. Professional breeders began their work and the first color variations came into existence. Yellow and white fish as well as those with black dots. At first a favourite of the nobility, the goldfish became popular and entered Chinese literature as a subject of many lyrical poems. About 1276 the period of domestication seems to have finished. In 1330 (Yüan-Dynasty), the goldfish came from southern parts of the land to Peking and from this point in time the care and breeding of the Chi-yu spread all over the country. Common people who could not afford their own goldfish pool kept at least some of these fish in a bowl or in some piece of earthenware pottery. Starting in 1546, Chinese poets were writing about goldfish in artistic bowls and not in pools anymore. Jade bowls were restricted to the upper class; less affluent people, whose favourite the goldfish had now become, continued to use earthenware pots.

By the end of the famous Ming-Dynasty (1368–1644) every household, whether rich or poor, had its goldfish bowl. After 1547, the majority of the varieties known today were already available. The development of the double caudal fin, the disappearance of the dorsal fin, the development of breeds like the celestial, the telescope, and the lionhead took place in the period between 1488–1726; after that, breeding varieties such as the Pearl Scale and other extreme forms followed.

From century to century, the goldfish

left: various forms of the fantail

42

became more and more popular in China. Many fancy breeds developed, showing the Chinese liking for the grotesque, the bizarre or even demonlike appearance. After fish culture became commonplace, the Chi-yu spread all over Asia. The first country which it appeared in, outside China, was Korea. It seems that here another breeding tendency developed, according to the different taste of the Korean people. Exact data about this change is unknown – one might, however, come to some conclusion when studying pictures and drawings from that period of time.

Around 1500, the goldfish came to Japan. The Japanese taste is completely different from the Chinese: it is similar to and more pleasing to the Western eye. One could say that Chinese taste is represented by the dragon, the Japanese by the cherry flower. Accordingly, Japanese goldfish breeds are charming, magnificent creatures, almost swimming flowers, which have to be looked at from above. The Japanese did not only import the goldfish; very soon they had their own hatcheries.

We known that between 1700 and 1710 a goldfish farm was established not far from Kyoto. In this area there still exists a hatchery today, founded in 1763. Because of their innate patience and perseverance, Japanese breeders managed to create and develop new varieties. When the Mandarin culture declined, the cultivation of the goldfish in China also declined; at the same time, the Japanese became the leading breeders of goldfish. Their fish soon became popular all over the world.

right: the oranda (with its cap) also comes in many forms

43

The Goldfish in the U.S. and Europe

Together with Marco Polo, the European explorer, reports about a striking fish from China reached Europe. It is quite possible that with James I (1566–1625) on the throne in Britain, the first live goldfish reached England. And only a fish as hardy as the goldfish would tolerate the endless and troublesome journey by sailing ship around the Cape of Good Hope.

The year 1691 is handed down to us as an authenticated date for the goldfish's arrival in Portugal (via Macao), followed in 1728 by an import from China by Mr. Philip Worth. Somewhat later, in the middle of the 18th century, the goldfish entered France. It came from China and was a present made to Madame de Pompadour. This lady was originally known as Antoinette Poisson (which means fish). Maybe the donors had their own thoughts about this present!

In the warm climates of Italy and Portugal, goldfish imports soon escaped became wild again and spread naturally.

Goldfish from Japan (rather than China) reached Europe later. English and European hatcheries began to breed from these imports. The first successful breeders in Europe were the Germans. Their fish were of a high standard. In 1870, Chr. Wagner's hatchery in Oldenburg had more than 60 pools for the cultivation of goldfish. In 1880, the Italians entered the goldfish market, where they established large hatcheries near Bologna. Favoured by the climate, their undertakings prospered, enabling them to sell their fish at moderate prices. Even today they are among the leading breeders and exporters of European goldfish.

Above we refer only to the plain goldfish and not to the many variations which are also available. In 1872, Paul Carbonnier brought some varieties to Paris (they were said to be from Japan, but more probably

Various forms of telescope-eyed goldfish

44

came from China) that created a sensation because of the body and fin structure. In 1883, Paul Matte-Lankwitz introduced the first Japanese long-finned goldfish to Germany.

Japanese, living in Berlin, had talked about a peculiar golden fish with veil-like fins. Paul Matte contacted a German company in Japan. They bought some specimens and put them into the special care of a captain for the long journey to Europe. This first shipment was a complete failure. The second comprised of 260 specimens: only 28 tiny fish arrived in Hamburg in the autumn of 1883. They were more dead than alive. In 1885, however, Matte received 24 excellent specimens after having promised a prize for their safe arrival. By careful breeding, the famous "Matte strain" was developed. Through many generations these fish kept their significant feature: excellent fins. In the year of 1950, I saw some fish in Berlin that unmistakably still showed the characteristic structure of the famous Matte strain.

In 1878, Rear Admiral Daniel Ammon brought the first fish from Far East to the U.S. and gave them to the United States Fish Commissioner. Fish breeders at the Governmental Hatchery in Washington continued their cultivation. Subsequently private hobbyists imported large quantities of Japanese goldfish as well as European breeds. Today, the U.S. and Japan have the largest goldfish hatcheries in the world. I would like to mention here the fish farms in Frederick County, Maryland; Martinsville, Indiana; Thornburg, Iowa; Langdon, Kansas. In Frederick County one hatchery was started in 1889; some few years later the number had grown to 35 and finally rose to 40 with hundreds of employees. In 1924, these farms supplied between 3 and 4 million goldfish. At present, approximately 19 different varities are cultivated there.

celestial   bubble-eye   pearl scale

The subsequent rise in popularity of exotic tropical fishes sent the goldfish back into the outdoor pool; the bizarre breeds were condemned by tropical fish fans. The veiltail, the telescope-eye and other variations were regarded as almost deformed monsters, as cripples. If this is so then, all breeds of dogs could be rejected, with the exception of the wolf and the jackal. In reality, however, the different forms and breeds are most interesting creatures, which will broaden our knowledge far more than many wild fish. With regard to tropical fish: have we not started to develop "cripples" and unusual strains as well?

General and Selective Breeding of Goldfish

After hibernating in a cool but frost-free place and after coming into breeding condition, fish of the outdoor pool will start their spawning activities one sunny day in a shallow part of the pool. If properly maintained, goldfish may be mature by the age of 10 months: the experienced breeder, however, will not use them before they are 2 years old.

Depending on the temperature, the spawning period starts in March and ends in August. Mature breeders are easy to tell. When looked at from the side, the anal region of the male is slightly concave, while the female's is slightly convex. During the spawning period, the male's gill covers and the first spines of the pectoral fins are covered with the so-called bright, knot-like dots ("tubercles"), while the female becomes heavy-bodied. Only beautiful specimens should be selected for breeding, fish with a faultless body structure and intense colors, and especially those, which changed their colors at an early age (at least by the age of 2 or 3 months). Only these specimens guarantee that their off-spring – or at least 95 % – will change colors, too.

It is not difficult to induce goldfish to spawn in a tank. However, this container has to offer sufficient swimming space; most of all, it has to be long. At least two males should be put together with one mature female. The bottom of the spawning container should be covered with delicate plant cushions: Java Moss, *Nitella, Myriophyllum (Elodea* is less suited), or with a layer of synthetic wool, which is more generally used today. The plants should be fastened to small stones or gravel, or weighted down with weights.

On a sunny day after violent chasing, spawning activities will start in the early morning hours and will culminate about noon. Large quantities of eggs are ejected, which will swirl around in the entire tank due to the excessive movements of the parents. As goldfish are voracious egg eaters they should be removed immediately after the procedure is finished. The sexes should be separated, too, as the male will not stop chasing the female.

The raising of the delicate young (that hatch after 5–7 days) is not difficult. As the small fry grow rapidly and are quite voracious feeders, they should be fed according to an old Chinese rule: with the hard-boiled yellow of an egg, finely sieved. Crushed *Daphnia* or *Tubifex* are also suitable. These foods, however, have the disadvantage of adding substances to the tank that might foul the water. Modern dry foods do not have this disadvantage; they are of a high nutritional value and promote fish growth.

In the outdoor pool, the development of the fry has to be left to nature. Quite a number of young will, however, develop. The breeding method of goldfish farms is the same as with carp. Potential breeders are carefully "milked" by hand in order to obtain the largest possible quantity of fertilized eggs.

The most important factor when using this method is to use only mature fish. Males and females should be kept separate. The only difficulty is that most of the time there are not sufficient males at hand!

However, this may be attempted as follows: If a mature pair is available, first one then the other fish should be taken up in such a way that the anal opening comes to lie just under the water surface. By a careful stroking from the fish's head to the vent alongside the belly eggs and a milky-white fluid are ejected into the water where they should be mixed together. For this purpose the hobbyist should use containers with an approximate capacity of 2 litres – which should be emptied into the outdoor pool where the eggs and young will develop by themselves. Like this it is possible to hatch more than 1 hundred thousand from one pair.

Smaller fish hatcheries in the U.S. and Japan use concrete pools for breeding purposes. Most of the time the breeder selects two females and three males, in large pools as many males as females. Breeding time in Japan is from the beginning of April until the middle of May. According to Matsubara the success depends on the proper feeding and maintenance in the months of September, October and November of the preceeding year. During this period of time the fish should be abundantly fed with live food. At breeding time the sexes are separated; no more fresh water is added to their tanks. Approximately 10 days before spawning fish are fed an abundant quantity of mosquito larvae, *Tubifex*, and earthworms. The exact day is selected by the breeder: the water of the spawning pool is completely renewed the day before. After that the potential breeders are added. The bottom should be covered with *Myriophyllum*. The majority of spawnings will occur the next morning.

After consuming their own egg yolk, the fry should be fed further with the hardboiled yellow of an egg, mixed with water and finely sieved. (Two yolks of a chicken's egg should be mixed with approximately 10 cm^3 or two teaspoons of water.) This mixture has to be of a uniform yellow color before it is added to the tank. After seven days of yolk feeding, the young fish should be offered small crustaceans (finely sieved *Daphnia*) for the next 15 days, followed by mosquito larvae and earthworms. *Artemia* larvae are actually the best food for the young offspring; it is, however, not inexpensive.

If the hobbyist wants to do what the experts call "selective breeding", it is recommended to use small tanks that are easily observed. According to this Japanese method, young fish that change their colors first, are separated to serve as a stock for further spawnings. If this is done repeatedly, the hobbyist will finally have a stock that is almost guaranteed 100% to change colors quite early on in their life. If, on the other hand, the young are left to

themselves, the percentage of wild forms will increase.

The Breeding and Rearing of Different Goldfish Varieties

Breeding techniques for the various fancy goldfish varieties are just the same as described previously. It is recommended to use tanks, as careful selection has to take place.

Most varieties will react as the normal goldfish does. A strict selection of potential breeders is even more important. The offspring have to be selected again and again as soon as the fins begin to divide. Even when using this breeding technique, there will appear plain and unchanged fish from time to time, which have the advantage of being hardier than the fancy varieties. The better the breeding stock, the larger the number of fish of good quality. A breeding stock of inferior quality will always result in a low percentage of first rate fish. To breed fish requires an experienced hand, and it takes time to gain experience. Breeds, as for example the telescope-eye and the celestial require most attentive breeding: when breeding the telescope it might happen that not even one single specimen among the offspring is of the same appearance as the parents.

When spawning, these quiet animals become so vivid and active that it is almost unbelievable. During the process of spawning, short intervals of rest occur and it is recommended then to remove the plants on which eggs have been deposited, or to cover them, as the parents are egg eaters if given the opportunity. When the fish remain completely quiet and exhausted on the tank bottom, showing no interest in each other, the spawning is finished and the parents should be removed. The raising of the young should be carried out as described before. It is recommended to start the first selection after two weeks. If observed from above, it is possible to distinguish between double-finned specimens and those with single fins, which are larger most of the time. After two more weeks inferior specimens among the double-finned fish should be removed. At this time, fish of first rate quality are easily recognized by a regular disposition of the fins and a short but attractive general anatomy. These specimens should receive the most careful attention of the hobbyist.

These small fish require lots of oxygen, good aeration and a frequent water change. Special attention has to be paid to the temperature and the quality of the water. The fertility of the double-finned breeds is essentially lower than that of the hardier forms. Depending on the size of the female, approximately one thousand eggs are ejected; when breeding the telescope-eye, the result might be less. As these varieties suffer from defects in vision – most of the time they are extremely short-sighted – the fertilization of the deposited eggs is extremely difficult; the "milking method" is not easily carried out because of their short, rounded bodies. Apart from that, by using this process, the protruding eyes might easily be damaged. It is therefore recommended to use a larger number of males for one female. – Only after three months is the development of the eyes detectable and only after this period of time should a selection take place. When selecting too early, it might happen that the best fish which develop late are inadvertently removed.

The most fascinating, for the professional breeder as well as the hobbyist, is the variety of breeding possibilities at hand. Apart from the strains which already exist, it is possible to combine the different strains: a game of chance in which the Chinese and the Japanese were masters because of their infinite patience. The experienced breeder will ascertain the following. Among the offspring of potential breeders there will always be so-called "comets", fish with an elongated, veil-like but single caudal fin. If the anatomy and the structure of the rest of the fins coincide with the double-finned parents, male comets are excellently suited for the breeding of double-finned specimens of high quality, as they are more vivid and active than the double-finned species, of which only the females are suited for breeding. Of course, the hobbyist should only use those comets descended from double-finned parents of first rate condition, not those with the elongated anatomy of the wild form, as this

would spoil the anatomy of the new offspring.

With these goldfish varieties anything is interchangeable and the numer of possible combinations and cross-breedings is almost inexhaustible. The following parts of the fish may be altered by selective breeding: the body itself, fins (length, form, and number), eyes, gill covers, mouth, nostrils, head, scales (size, number, and form), color.

Diseases and their Treatment

It seems quite natural that domesticated breeds such as the goldfish are especially susceptible to many diseases. The original form was – as we learn from history – a tough character – in spite of endless journeys, in spite of almost impossible conditions for life, the goldfish is still thriving.

Chilling

The different goldfish varieties are very susceptible to sudden chills, which will cause damage to the skin and the fins. Open wounds will be attacked by the fungus *Saprolegnia,* which gives them a whitish appearance. Diseased fish should be immediately moved from the affected tank to another, and gradually acclimated to a steady temperature of 24°C or above. A spoonful of salt per every 15–20 litres of tank water as well as **AquaSafe** should be added.

The wounds should be given special treatment out of the water by brushing them with a strong solution of potassium permanganate. This disease is frequently seen in the spring, when fish are placed into the outdoor pool and it is still too cold for them, as goldfish do not tolerate sudden temperature changes. Fancy breeds with their large, veil-like fins are even more susceptible.

Such a chilling may cause a disturbance in the swim bladder, the so-called "swim bladder disease". Diseased fish lie on the bottom of the tank, their movements are uncontrolled, they might even float belly-up along the water surface. Warmth and shallow water is absolutely necessary for fish that suffer from this disease. After a severe attack, some species do not get rid of their deformed, blown-up belly for the rest of their life.

Diseases of the Skin and the Fins

Transparent veil-like fins of some varieties might suddenly show blood streaks in the fin substance. This may be due to chilling, too strong aeration or too hard water. These effusions of blood will disappear soon after normal conditions have been re-established. Predatory insects may cause these blood streaks, too, and special attention should be paid to this when using live foods.

If the blood streaks do not disappear and the fins start to look ragged, the fish is probably severely attacked by ectoparasites: either *Ichthyophthirius, Costia* or *Gyrodactylus.* "Ich" is easily recognized: masses of white dots cover skin and fins. Other external parasites cause the skin to take on a slimy appearance with the fish's skin showing large, milky spots. Both diseases are caused by heavy parasite infestations. They may ruin fish farms, as the young fish are among those attacked. Larger specimens should be isolated. The water temperature of the quarantine tank should be raised to a minimum of 25°C and a treatment with special remedies should be started. It is recommended to change the water after 3 days and to repeat the whole procedure. If severely attacked, this treatment should be repeated until the fish are clean and their wounds begin to heal. Small fish may be treated in the pond or set-up tank.

Intestinal Diseases

After being fed bread, fish cake or other unsuitable dry food, fish may start to suffer from enteritis which will appear in the form of constipation. Under normal conditions, fish excrement is dark; if it is slimy, bloody or white, the fish is suffering from enteritis. Gas bubbles in a slimy excrement and a swollen body indicate that the fish is also suffering from an internal problem. In such a case, the temperature should be raised immediately and sea-salt should be added to the tank. After changing the water, the addition of **AquaSafe** is necessary.

When offering your fish lots of live food and a good vegetable diet or a special mixture containing vegetable substances, these diseases will not occur, or at least very rarely.

Poorly oxygenated, dirty water may be the cause of the dangerous "dropsy". In the beginning, fantails show dark spots of an almost black-red coloration on the body surface near the anus. At this stage, an immediate water change, strong aeration and filtration as well as the adding of sea-salt will help. At a later time, a general swelling of the fish's body takes place. If the attack is severe, the swelling may cause a protrusion of the scales. A cure is not known, and the fish should be killed. Very old fish that have been used for breeding purposes might suffer from this disease without any obvious cause.

Together with imports of Koi and goldfish, the so-called anchor worms may invade the tank. Actually, these are not real worms but parasites of the genus *Lernaea.* Their head in shape of an anchor digs into the fish's body; these parasites prefer spots behind the ventral and pectoral fins or the dorsal fin and the eyes. *Lernaea* is easily detected: first of all the fish reacts with a swollen reddish inflammation; apart from that the thread-like body of the parasite hangs freely outside the fish's body.

If not treated immediately, a mass development of this parasite will take place. The most secure treatment is the following: the parasite's body has to be cut off where it emerges from the fish's body. The part that remains in the fish's body will die off and is rejected. Apart from that anchor worms can be removed by the potassium permanganate method (short baths in a solution of 1 g per 10 litres or 26 U.S. galls of water for a time of 1–2 minutes).

Senility

The author would like to mention the following about the age of fish. I have a picture of a Japanese oranda from 1924: this fish, owned by the Japanese baron Yanagisawa, originating from his goldfish hatchery in Kariyama was 19 (!) years old and looked quite remarkable. From China it is reported that some specimens have reached the age of 40 years.

Further information on the diseases of goldfish and their treatments may be found in some of the books listed at the end of this book. A local vet or an experienced hobbyist can offer invaluable assistance in diagnosing and successfully treating diseased fish.

Different Goldfish Varieties

Group A

The structure of the fish's body resembles the wild form, the coloration is always different, fins might be partly different.

1. The Common Goldfish

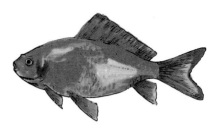

All parts of the body correspond to the wild form, no alterations or changes to the fins. Only the coloration is different. There are entirely white fish with a rosy shimmer, others with a mother-of-pearl shimmer. The common goldfish may also be grey, brown, gold, yellow, orange, and crimson or brass-colored. These colorations may be spotted with black and white dots. White and reddish-white breeds may develop "naked forms" with very thin scales. The most desirable species are deep-red breeds with complete scaling.

A very large, deep-red variation, showing the same characteristics as the common goldfish, is called "Wakin". This fish is very popular in the U.S.A. Originally, "Wakin" was the Japanese name for the original goldfish.

Various colour forms of the goldfish

2. Shubunkin or Calico Goldfish

3. Comet Goldfish

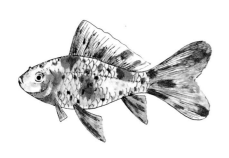

The body structure is like that of the common goldfish, the single caudal fin is greatly enlarged. When classifying this caudal fin, it is important that the spines run horizontally at least half of the caudal fin length, before they are bent downwards by the weight of the fin. Anal and ventral fins are elongated.

4. Fantail Goldfish

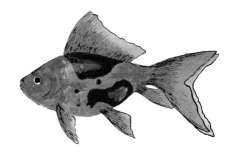

Very often the common goldfish is called shubunkin by mistake. Around 1900, this name was given to a goldfish variation in Japan with a variety of colors but without changes of the body structure. Japanese "Demekins", a breed with eye deviations, are known for their bight colors: violet or cinnabar fish with black dots (peppered with black). Wakins with red, white, blueish, and black spots were cross-bred with the above mentioned Demekins. By back-crossing, the color variations of the shubunkin developed. The original shubunkin is streamlined; it does not have doubled fins but an enlarged dorsal fin as well as a deeply notched enlarged caudal fin. The most extraordinary feature, however, is the mixture of colors of the body with transparent, uncolored scales.

The ground color is said to be a mixture of yellow, red, blue, and violet, spotted with small dots of black, white, red, brown, blue, violet, and yellow. The intensity of the different colors may vary from specimen to specimen. An absolute rarity are the almost entirely violet fish.

The body structure is like that of the common goldfish; caudal and anal fins, however, are doubled and have the same form as the veiltail goldfish. This variety is always entirely scaled. The body of the fantail goldfish may be shorter than that of the common goldfish, it may have a strong, unbent caudal peduncle. The fantail has an erect dorsal fin, a doubled anal fin, a broad, but not very long caudal fin, which is divided into two parts and never hangs down but is horizontally stretched out. The four different parts of the fin are deeply notched. The caudal fin should be longer than the fish itself and never have a veil-like appearance. Colors are similar to the fringetail goldfish.

Group B
Variations of the fish's body and the majority of the fins.

1. Nymph Goldfish

The nymph goldfish is closely related to the fringetail. From time to time, nymph goldfish appear among fringetail breeds. Under selective breeding, U.S. fish farmers used to remove the nymph goldfish and raise it separately.

The body of the nymph goldfish is very short, the caudal fin strong and long and similar to the comet's. Size and coloration may vary.

2. Fringetail Goldfish, Ryukin

The body of this very popular variety is short and almost spherical. The caudal fin is doubled and at least as long as the fish's body. But only if the caudal fin has attained the double length of the entire fish's body, does it become really precious. The flowing caudal fin is really attractive and floates in a wave-like manner. The brim of the caudal fin-halves, which should be separated at least to the middle, may be deeply forked or slightly dented (veiltail or broadtail). The four ends of the two caudal fin parts should be absolutely symmetrical; their ends should not be pointed, but slightly rounded off.

Varieties with a three cornered tail, i.e. where the halves have grown together in the middle and do not show distinct points, are called fantails or peacock-tails. They are considered to be of inferior quality.

The spines of the caudal fin should never be rigid but thin and flexible so that it really looks like a veil. If the fish does not move, the tail has to hang down. When moving, however, the appearance should be wave-like. The longer the ventral and pectoral fins and the higher the dorsal fin, the more valuable the fish. The elongated anal fin has to be paired. Length, form, and structure of the fins determine the fish's quality. The posterior spines of the dorsal fin for example have to be longer than the caudal peduncle, the pectoral fins should by far surpass the ventral fins, whereas the ventral fins should surpass the starting point of the anal fin. The base of the anal fin, however, has to be covered by parts of the tail. The length of the anal fin has to be half the length of the caudal fin.

The Japanese breeders did an excellent job when creating this rarity; small bodies, veiled by infinite fin masses, with brilliant, delicate colors. The Japanese name "Ryukin" is derived from Ryu-Kyu or Lu-Chu-Islands between Formosa and the Japanese Islands, which may indicate the route the wild form took under its introduction from China.

Normally the fringetail is completely scaled; those without scales are rarer and more precious.

Their coloration may differ: a brilliant, shining red, however, is the proper color of this variety, which might even shimmer metallically. Species without scales might be white or red-spotted, with a blue or black iris; seldomly do these varieties show black or blue-dotted bodies. The most beautiful and most precious color variation, however, is the red one. Entirely black examples are very rare; the grey-colored wild forms are not interesting for the breeder. Recently, copper-colored variations have appeared on the market.

A valuation of the Ryukin should always be made with regard to the structure of the fins and the shape of the body, the scaling, and a brilliant, intensive coloration.

3. Veiltail, Broadtail

The veiltail is a breeding variety of the fringetail, showing almost the same characteristic features. The extremely solid caudal fin is not dented, all fins have regular folds, the dorsal fin stands very upright and starts quite early, almost at the nape. The fish's body should appear as small and delicate as possible.

Group C
The fish's body is markedly deformed, the fins are in a process of regression.

1. Eggfish or Rancher

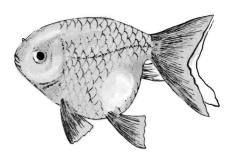

The body of this little fish is almost egg-like; there is no dorsal fin. It is said that this variety comes from Korea, where it is called Maruko or Ranchu. The eggfish is a very rare fish, which is not very popular. It has been bred from the fantail goldfish and like this fish it has a very short, but doubled caudal fin. The eggfish is brass-colored, white, or gold-spotted. Entirely white fish are very rare.

Not even traces of the dorsal fin should be seen in the eggfish; the back, however, has to be completely scaled. In relation to the length of the body, the eyes of the eggfish should be a little larger than those of the fantail.

2. Japanese Lionhead Goldfish

Even more than the eggfish, the lionhead goldfish shows the Chinese love for the monstrous, even the grotesque. Japanese breeders cultivated the lionhead, too, and today this fish might be called a perfect breed. In Japan the lionhead is called Shishigashira or Korean goldfish, which again might indicate its origin. The body of the lionhead is almost spherical. The head is short, but broad, and completely covered by wartlike exuberances, giving the lionhead its name. The coloration of the lionhead is remarkable. Monochromatic fish do not exist: body and fins may be red, the head showing another shade of red: pink, white, or cream; or the fish's body is white and the head and the fins are red. Another color variation has a white body with lines of brilliant red scales. In such cases, the head is pink-colored.

The movements of the lionhead are rather awkward: the missing dorsal fin makes balancing difficult. Some breeds are only able to swim on their backs, others with their heads down (in a "head-down" movement). The caudal fin is doubled but very small, most of the time, the lower halves are horizontally spread apart. The characteristic feature of this fish, the exuberances, appear during the second year of life and keep growing. Lionheads may be difficult to keep as they are very delicate. Perfect, beautiful lionheads are hardly obtainable at present. There were times when perfect lionheads were worth twenty times their weight in gold.

Group D
Combination of B2 and C2

1. Dutch Lionhead Goldfish, Oranda

In 1840, Japanese breeders managed to crossbreed lionheads and fringetails and they obtained a beautiful fish, the Oranda Shishigashira or Dutch lionhead. This species has nothing to do with Holland; but at that time it was quite common in Japan to call everything that was new or awkward as "Dutch"! The characteristic features of both parents show in the oranda.

The form of the body and the fins is that of the fringetail; the exuberances on the head come from the lionhead: they may be cap-like in this fish. The beautiful colors come from the lionhead, too. "Red Hoods" are very popular. Certain forms may develop to a considerable size.

When back-crossing the oranda with the lionhead, a new variety arises: the Shukin or fringetail lionhead. The characteristic features of the lionhead prevail here: body structure, dorsal fin missing, head exuberances. Existing fins are fully developed and as large as those of the fringetail. Contrary to the oranda, which is very popular nowadays, this variety is very rare.

2. Tiger-Head, Bouquet

This Chinese variety is derived from the oranda. No fin deviations, sometimes the forked veiltail may be rather small. Eyes and scales are normal. Characteristic fea-

tures of the tiger-head are bouquetlike head protruberences. Colorations: gold, yellow, cream as well as light brown.

Group E
Modified bodies, fins and eyes

1. Chinese Telescope-eyed Goldfish

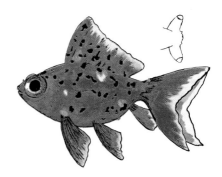

Apart from small deviations, the body form and the structure of the fins are similar to the fringetail. The characteristic feature of all telescope-eyed goldfish is the enlargement and projection of the eye with the result that the eyes of this fish jut forwards or to either side. The degree of enlargement as well as the form of the eye vary quite a lot. These kind of eyes develop relatively late. At the age of three to six months the hobbyist may detect the first signs, but only after 2–3 years has the development finished. It is not seldom that only one eye is "telescoped", the other may be normal. Together with these characteristic eyes, the telescope combines all features of the fringetail. The body of the telescope should be short and rounded off, the back should be relatively broad with a short head; the large eyes may pass over to the snout or even pass them. Apart from the dorsal fin, all other fins should not be too large. The caudal fin should be doubled but never hang.

Colorations: red, or white, or both. Most precious, however, are those forms that have other colors in irregular shades, dots, or stains: the Demekins. All these breeds with their enlarged eyes are extremely short-sighted. It may even be possible that they only can distinguish between light and dark. As a consequence they easily bump against the decoration material and hurt their delicate eyes so that finally they are blind. The best suited containers for the keeping of these fish are round ones without stones, only with soft plants.

The origin of the telescope-eyed goldfish is Chinese, they were not popular in Japan.

3. Veiltail Moor

2. Veiltail or Broadtail Telescope-eyed Goldfish

This fish is mostly the work of American breeders. The broadtail telescope-eye combines the characteristics of the veiltail with those of the Chinese Demekin or telescope-eye: specimens with perfect fins and bodies, no scales, regular, large eyes, and shubunkin coloration. Blue is the most important color in this fish.

The most perfect fish among all these breeding variations is the veiltail moor. The structure of the body as well as the fins is the same as in the broadtail telescope; the coloration of the veiltail moor, however, is of a deep velvet brown-black, covering the entire body, the fins, and the eyes. Only the belly may be bluish-grey or gold. Often the fins have a slight bronze shimmer. Pure strains should have a constant black coloration; it happens, however, that young moors with a perfect coloration turn into gold when adult. It is recommended to cross-breed a deep-red fish with a black one. Moors are completely scaled. It is noteworthy that the black coloration often goes together with telescope-eyes.

4. Celestial Telescope-eyed Goldfish   5. Bubble-Eye

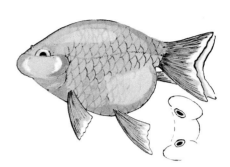

This fish is a typical Chinese breeding variety with its short, compact, and completely scaled body. The head is short with a blunt snout, the dorsal fin is missing, the short tail is doubled. In the beginning, the celestial shows the characteristic eye development of a telescope-eye. Later, however, the eyeballs turn upward so that this fish can see in one direction only. Formerly it was maintained that Chinese breeders kept the celestial in narrow, completely dark containers, just allowing one light ray from above to enter. Even in 1907, Mr. K. Stansch, a very experienced breeder, suggested the following method. When breeding the celestial it is recommended to cover the lateral glasses of the tank with dark paper so that the young fish get light only from above. Like this, they are forced to look up, which will have a favourable influence on the growth of the pupil.
Of course, this recommendation is absurd! Why should the fish look up at all? Breeds, showing all the characteristic features are very rare; in view of the fact that the special eye develops rather late.
Formerly a very rare fish, the celestial was hardly obtainable on the market. Mainly its color is described as reddish-gold. Recently, larger quantities have been imported from China. These imports, however, remained rather small, their grey color had a brass-like shimmer. Until now, breeding was impossible.

Body and fins are similar to the celestial; like this fish, the bubble-eye does not have a dorsal fin. Its eyes, however, differ completely from that of the celestial.
The eyes of the bubble-eye are not elongated. Around the eyes and especially under them we find a baggy formation, filled with liquid. When looked at superficially, the eyes remind us of the celestial: the bubble-eye's anatomy, however, is quite different. Authors, as for example Stansch and Smith, describe the bubble-eye as the most deformed aquarium fish because of the peculiar tilting of the eyes. Mr. J.J. Affleck, an English aquarist, wrote in 1953: "although these fish are without good vision, they can live very well in a community tank. After close observation it is difficult to believe that they have disadvantages because of their eyes. Fish seem to depend more on their chemical sense and the lateral line organ than on their eyes".
The author of this book has experienced the same. In spite of the missing dorsal fin − which makes it difficult for this fish to swim − they managed to escape from the net quite skilfully.

6. Dragon-Eye

2. Pearl-Scale

Lately, the dragon-eye has been offered in different color by Chinese breeders. This fish has all fins as well as scales, its physical appearance is egglike. Its eyes might be regarded as a first step to the telescope development. They are strongly developed and protrude in a button-like way. There are different color combinations: such as black, red, and dotted dragoneyes. Until now, this fish has seldomly been exported from Hong Kong.

The pearl-scale has all fins, the caudal fin as well as the anal fin are doubled. The scales protrude on the egg-like body; their brims are dark and may have the appearance of small shells, they may also be rounded off and look like pearls. A lost scale will be replaced by a plain one. The most popular colors of the pearl-scale are gold and orange. It is obtainable in England.

Group F
Other changes:

1. Pompon

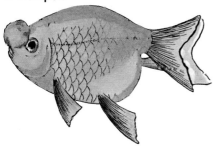

3. Curled Gill

The pompon is similar to the oranda and the lionhead; the characteristic feature, however, is a strongly enlarged, ball-like nose wrinkle. Chinese pompons are without dorsal fins; the nostrils are extremely large and have the appearance of balls of wool yarn. Until now, we know blue pompons, also called velvet pompons, as well as red pompons. They are occasionally exported to England.

Completely scaled, all scales having a normal form. Without dorsal fin, although some hybrids may have one. Otherwise similar to the egg-fish. The inner part of the gill cover is turned outwards. Like this, the gill filaments are visible.

Apart from the different breeds mentioned above, other combinations exist, for example a red dragon eye with the opercle turned outwards.

Cyprinus carpio – The Koi

Its History and Importance

Most probably Japanese breeders developed the colorful variations of this well-known carp. This fish is very popular in Japan and breeding it may be dated back to 500 a.d. By 300 years a.d. 5 different color variations had been recorded.

According to the opinion of todays ichthyologists, the carp comes originally from the waters of Japan and China. The English called it "fancy carp", the Japanese Nishikigoi, Higoi, or Irogoi. The Japanese common name for this fish is "Koi", which is also used in the U.S. "Koi" is not an abbreviation, but means "love". Although the carp is not a symbol for love, Japanese give it as a present to good friends, just as we give flowers.

Originally, the Japanese origin of the Koi is restricted to the Yamakoshi region in the Northern part of Middle Honshu. Although the climate is not very favourable – in winter the snow may be 5–7 m (20 feet) deep – Japanese breeders with their infinite patience began to create the Koi more than 1000 years ago.

During the winter, the breeders protected these precious fish in their own houses. The most careful attention was paid to them and they were treated like members of the family. Just as other domestic animals, Koi had their own special names which were known to the entire village.

Japanese Praise of the Koi

Even in this technical age, Koi are described with a great deal of enthusiasm. A Japanese dealer will offer a Koi in the following manner: "A freshwater fish which will become your sweetheart, with its brilliant colors and friendly nature. Its body may have just one color, it may be dotted or stained, showing at the same time different shades of purple, white, gold, etc. Although there are thousands of variations, the colors of each particular fish are distinct and will immediately catch your eye. Even more appealing are their gay, active, and rhythmic movements. The entire day they swim to and fro, moving their small transparent, fan-like pectoral fins, looking at you with their wise, round eyes and their large snouts. Watch them in bright light! Any sudden movement, any turn they make casts bright rays and their beauty is more than can be described. Perhaps you happen to see them in dim light and you pause because of these wonderful darkening colors that change at any moment. It is no exaggeration, but these really esthetic values cannot be described in words. It is best to look at these fish, they will give you new joy in life."

In Japan, there even lives a Koi poet. Dr. Takeo is a very popular and busy surgeon; his free time, however belongs to the Koi. He recovers from the stress of his profession when meditating near his wonderful Koi pool. Perhaps the following poem resulted from one of these quiet moments:

Green shades, forbidden depth, small waves curl the water surface and below them the shimmer of the Koi.

Whoever found similar words for the "neon fish" in the Western part of the world, without running the risk of making a fool of himself?

According to an old custom, on the 5th of May the Japanese hoist Koi, made of paper or silk, in order to implore success in life for their sons. In older times the Koi was regarded as a royal bringer of luck.

Maintenance and Types of Koi

In the past, Japanese breeders only showed the Koi occasionally at international exhibitions. In 1963, at the international show in Hamburg, they exhibited a fantastic collection. In England as in Japan this fish is very popular, being kept in pools and also successfully bred now. Unfortunately, the Koi is fully grown in a short time,

which makes them unsuitable for the indoor tanks. They are, therefore, better kept in pools.

Such a pool should not be too small; when offered on the market, Koi are approximately 10–20 cm (4–8 ins.) in size. Very soon they will attain a length of 45 cm (18 ins.). Pools of less than 4 m (12 feet) long are therefore not recommended.

The water level has to be less than 2 m (6 feet), as otherwise these fish are hardly to be seen as they prefer the lower water regions. They will eat anything edible and constantly stir up the bottom.

Artificial foods, commonly used by today's fish keepers, are very practical and accepted by the Koi. It is, however, recommended to feed them sparingly and to offer live food whenever possible.

In winter, the Koi has to be kept in a frost-free place: a cellar, for example, or – as in England – in heated open air pools. As mentioned before, Koi should not be kept in deep frost-free garden ponds, as the hobbyist might then hardly detect them in summer because they live in the lower water regions.

The value of each Koi depends largely on its coloration: It might fetch more than 1,000 U.S. dollars. When spotted breeds are concerned, the value will be dependent on the size and the localisation of the colored dots; the ground color is important, too. Their often poetical names are given them in view of the following points:

1. from the coloration a certain fish has.
2. from nature: trees, flowers, animals, mountains, or the sky.
3. from the place of breeding or the date of creation, for example, in which dynasty.

As all these names may be combined as well, they might confuse the Western hobbyist, if he does not understand a little of the Japanese mentality.

In order to explain the principle, the author would like to mention some Koi names, which are often to be found in Japanese price lists:

One-colored Koi

Metallic Ohgon Koi with a silvery, golden, yellowish, orange or platinum shimmer. Unmixed colors.

Two-colored Koi

Kohaku   white with red markings.
Hi Utsuri   black with red patches.
Shiro Bekko   white with black markings.
Shushui   blue back and shoulders, red belly.

Three-colored Koi

Sanshoku   white, red and black (many variations).
Asagi   bright or pale blue. Back with bright blue scales, red marks; the scales have a white brim.

Care and Feeding Table

for the Successful Care of the Most Popular

Cold-Water Fish

Revised by Hans A. Baensch

Scientific name / Common name	Amount of Care Required	Amount of Oxygen Required (l, m, h) / Temperature ☆	Size of Adult Fish in cm	Minimum Tank Size in cm	TetraFin in Your Tank	Dorofin or TetraFin in Your Garden Pond	TetraMin, Conditioning Food for Small Tank Fish / TabiMin	TabiMin for Fish up to 7 cm in Length ●	Foodsticks or pellets for Fish of more than 15 cm ○	Live Food
European Cold-Water Fish										
Alburnoides bipunctatus — Scheider	▣	h	10-14	80	A	A				
Leuciscus idus — Orfe	▣	m ☆	15-30	100	A	A	T		●	
Misgurnus fossilis — Weather loach	□	l ☆	15-30	80	A	A		●	●	
Phoxinus phoxinus — Minnow	■	h ☆	10	100	A	A	T			L
Rhodeus amarus — Bitterling	▣	m ☆	5–7	60	A	A	⊘ T			L
Rutilus rutilus — Roach	□	m	25-30	100	A	D			●	
Scardinius erythrophthalmus — Rudd	▣	m ☆	20-30	100	A	D	⊘		○	
Tinca tinca — Tench	□	l ☆	20-30	100	A	D	⊘	●	●	
Gasterosteus aculeatus — 3-spined stickleback	■	m ☆	7-9	60			T			L
Pungitius pungitius — 9-spined stickleback	▣	m ☆	3-6	50			T			L
North American Cold-Water Fish										
Centrarchus macropterus — Flier	▣	h	12-16	100			T			L
Elassoma evergladei — Dwarf sunfish	▣	l ★	3	40			T			L Artemia
Enneacanthus obesus — Diamond sunfish	■	h	6-10	80			T			L
Ictalurus nebulosus — Brown bullhead	□	l	15-45	100	A	A		●	●	
Lepomis species	■	h	15-22	100			T			L
Mesogonistius chaetodon — Black-banded sunfish	■	h	10	80			T			L
Umbra pygmaea — Eastern mudminnow	□	l	10	80			T			L
Asiatic Cold-Water Fish										
Carassius auratus — Goldfish	□	l ★	15-35	100	A	D			○	
Carassius auratus — Fancy goldfish	□	l ★	12-20	80	A	A		○	○	
Cyprinus carpio — Koi	▣	l ★	30-50	120	A	D			●	
Tanichthys albonubes — White-cloud mountain minnow	□	m ★	4	60			T			
Zacco platypus	▣	m	15	80	A	A	T	○	●	

Explanation of the Care and Feeding Table

This table is the result of practical research and makes the basic requirements of 20 of the most popular cold-water fish known to the hobbyist at a glance. The species mentioned are relatively easy to keep and therefore especially suited for the novice aquarist. The table deals with each fish under the following headings:

Fish Names

In scientific circles only the Latin name has validity. The names mentioned in this table should help the beginner to acquaint himself with the English common names.

Amount of Care Required

The data in this column has been gathered by practical research. They comprise indications as regards the water quality, the compatibility, the feeding, the adaptation to temperature. This information will help the aquarist to select fish and to avoid unnecessary disappointment.

The symbols mean:

☐ Hardy species, normal water requirements, no feeding problems. Suited for cold-water community tanks, unless the differences in size with other fish are too large.

▣ Hardy species; normal water requirements (water hardness 10–20° GH; pH 7–7.5).

▣ More attention must be given to the oxygen supply. Attentive, careful feeding. Only suited for the community tank with care. Sunfish, for example, should not be trusted in the community with smaller fish as they regard them as prey.

■ Not recommended for the beginner. Special requirements in feeding: during the first weeks of tank life, only live foods are accepted. Fish for aquarists who have live foods at their disposal all the time.

Amount of Oxygen Required

The letters in this column indicate the following:

l = low oxygen levels
If your tank is not too crowded (1 cm of fish per 5 litres of water) (1 ins to 2.5 U.S. gallons) no aeration is required. Filtration is, however, recommended because it will keep the water clean and clear.

m = medium oxygen levels
An air pump or an air stone is necessary in addition to the filter equipment if the water temperature exceeds 19°C (66°F).

h = high oxygen levels
These fish species come from cool clear mountain streams which are fairly well-oxygenated. In addition to an effective filter, they require strong aeration. Most of the time, these species do not tolerate a water temperature of more than 20°C (68°F).

Temperature Required

The data in the column headed "Amount of Oxygen Required" carry either a red or blue asterisk.

☆ The blue asterisk indicates those species which can tolerate temperatures below 15°C. Those fish hibernate in the outdoor pool, if the oxygen supply is sufficient. Feed the fish sparingly if the water temperature is below 15°C and do not feed them at all when the temperature is below 12°C (53°F). Higher temperature than 20°C (68°F) are not tolerated well.

✶ The red asterisk shows that the species in question can tolerate water temperatures of more than 20°C (up to a maximum of 24°C or 75°F) if additional aeration is provided.

Average Size of Adult Fish

If the hobbyist buys young or nearly adult fish, this column aids in planning by giving the average size in cm of adult fish of each species. The first number indicates the size this species will attain in a tank; the second number indicates the size it will attain in its natural environment. To convert cm to ins, multiply by 0.39.

Minimum Tank Size

These data have been proven in practice. A good-sized tank will always be less trouble than a smaller one. Remember that 100 cm is approximately equal to one yard (three feet).

Feeding Plan for Outdoor Pools

The aquarist should feed his pool fish at least twice daily. In addition, there is always some live food at their disposal: mosquito larvae, algae and *Daphnia* (if the pond is large enough). Starting in April, when the water has reached a temperature of approximately 16°C (61°F), the hobbyist should feed his pets. Feed sparingly from the month of September and stop in October if the water temperature is below 12°C (54°F). Fish hardly feed now until the following spring.

Feeding Plan for Aquarium Fish

The hobbyist is referred to page 12.

Feeding Plan

This column indicates the correct food for the species in question.

Bold letters indicate the main diet, which should be fed 2–4 times per day, depending on the pool or aquarium temperature. Apart from that, additional foods have been indicated, to offer your fish additional valuable nutrition and some variety of diet.

Feed your fish carefully! High temperatures increase their appetite, lower temperatures make it decrease. Most cold-water species require more food than the smaller species of the warm water tank because of their larger body size! Do not overfeed your fish. Never feed them more than will be eaten within 2–3 minutes (dry food) or 1 hour (live food). However, at a water temperature of 20°C (68°F) or more, fish should be fed more frequently than twice per day. Otherwise they will grow thin or become diseased due to nutritional deficiencies.

When fed properly, fish can do without food one day per week. And it will not harm your fish if they have to do without food for a weekend or so.

Cold-water fish can live on a feeding device while you are on vacation, if they have been accustomed to dry food. If not, they should be moved into the outdoor pool. If not fed additionally for 3–4 weeks, your fish can live on algae and insects – for example, while you are on holiday.

Food requirements of cold-water fish vary according to their native habitat and way of life. Carp-like fish will eat just about everything, sunfish from North America prefer live food. If they accept dry food, they should be offered **TetraMin Large Flakes** instead of **TetraFin** which has a high vegetable content. **TetraMin** on the other hand has a high animal content.

T **TetraMin Basic Food.** Any aquarist should have **TetraMin Basic Food** at hand, unless he exclusively keeps goldfish and their different varieties. These fish will not tolerate **TetraMin** as it contains too much protein. For all other fish, **TetraMin** is the basic food and contains vitamins and other nutrients, especially for those species that prefer animal food.

For a short period of time, the flakes float on the water surface; after they have been dipped they sink slowly to the tank bottom. Therefore, every fish can reach them and it does not matter whether the tank inhabitants prefer the upper, medium, or lower water regions.

It is best to use **TetraMin Large Flakes** if your fish have attained a size of more than 7 cm. Never directly shake the food from the can into the tank. This should be avoided in any case as the feeding portion may be too large.

Although **TetraMin** does not cloud the water, too much food in the tank promotes the proliferation of bacteria. It is therefore recommended to take a pinch of food out of the can and to spread this quantity on the water surface. Another possibility is as follows: an established feeding quantity should be poured into the tank out of the cap of the drum.

TetraMin Large Flakes should be put between two fingers and dipped gently under the water surface. Fish will then come and feed right out of your hand.

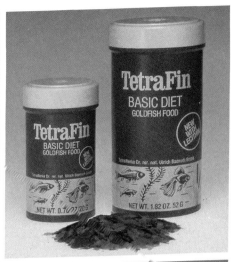

✍ **Tetra Conditioning Food** should be fed just as **TetraMin**. This food is especially suited for plant feeding fish, as it contains less protein and fats. As an additional diet it may be given to all cold-water fish that accept it. Fish that have reached the size of approximately 7 cm should be fed **Tetra Conditioning Food Large Flakes**, smaller ones should be given **Tetra Conditioning Food**.

🅰 🅰 **TetraFin** is the main diet for goldfish and all carp-like cold-water fish. Vitamins and the necessary trace elements, a lower protein content and a high content of carbohydrates make **TetraFin** the right food to strengthen your fish for the long winter and to tempt them to leave their hiding places in spring. **TetraFin** contains raw materials that young goldfish up to approximately 12 cm in size require for healthy growth. Due to the high vitamin content, fish will easily spawn in spring. Due to its highly nutritious ingredients and the fact that it will not foul the water, **TetraFin** is the right food for the fish species mentioned, especially when kept in tanks.

D D **DoroFin** should be fed as an additional diet to **TetraFin**. This food does not contain fats but other inert materials. The albumen content is low, the content of carbohydrates is high. **DoroFin** is an inexpensive and valuable addition to **TetraFin** and the natural pool food as insects, larvae, and sometimes *Daphnia*. This food is especially suitable for feeding pool fish in summer, from May to August.

As goldfish were thought to have no special requirements, they were offered bread, flaked oats, shrimp waste as well as the so-called Japanese fish cake. As the goldfish is very modest, it will stay alive. It will, however, not grow in a healthy manner and will refuse to spawn. If you really like your fish you should use those foods that have been developed scientifically for cold-water fish. It promotes their health and secures a long life for them.

O● **TabiMin** is a tablet food and therefore offers a food source to those fish living in the lower regions of your tank. **TabiMin** is a mixture composed of **TetraMin** and **Tetra Conditioning Food** and is therefore suitable for fish that feed on plant or animal materials. Fish which only accept live food will accept **TabiMin**, too.

O● Pellets and/or TetraPond Foodsticks
In many countries there are special goldfish pellets obtainable on the market. In addition, **Tetra** have now developed the concept of highly nutritious foodsticks for fish. These float for many hours and may be used to form a balanced, staple diet for all pond fish, especially Koi. Because there is less waste, **Tetra Foodsticks** are even preferred to flaked foods for pond fish, and are more nutritious than most pellet foods.

Live Food   L L
Feeding live food in the show tank may be dangerous. Fish diseases may invade the tank, especially when *Daphnia* and some mosquito larvae are fed. Live food from waters that do not contain fish are therefore preferable. The most important live food is *Daphnia* which is very valuable because of its vitamin content even if it does have a low nutritous value otherwise. They should

only be used in case of emergency for a few days. When feeding live food, the hobbyist should bear in mind that "variety is the spice of life". Fish like to have changes from time to time.

Artemia, Brine Shrimp
Young fish, until they have attained a size of more than 6 cm (2–3 ins.), can be fed *Artemia*. For the cultivation of brine shrimp, the hobbyist needs an air pump, a bottle, a 1 % salt solution and the eggs. The small brine shrimps are a most popular diet for all small fish. Fish hatcheries all over the world use them. *Artemia* have the important advantage of being virtually disease free. The hobbyist who wants to breed coldwater fish should use this excellent live food.

Red Mosquito Larvae
This is the best live food for the aquarium fish mentioned in this booklet. Many dealers offer deep-frozen red mosquito larvae. These frozen foods have to be fed very sparingly, as the remains decay and will foul the water. Frozen foods have the advantage that diseases are not so easily transmitted as with live food.

Black Mosquito Larvae
These are obtainable from spring to fall in still waters. After a short period of time, mosquitoes will hatch from their larvae. Therefore, the hobbyist should not feed more black mosquito larvae than the fish will eat. Otherwise, mosquitoes will invade his room!

Tubifex
They live in poorly-oxygenated waters. They should only be used in case of emergency. They burrow under the tank bottom and many die there. Fish, exclusively fed on *Tubifex*, will soon have a dangerous surplus of fat in their liver.

Earth Worms
Larger fish (more than 10 cm or 4 ins.) like red earth worms as they have a high protein content. It might, however, turn out to be difficult for the aquarist to obtain earth worms regularly. Some sunfish species will accept chopped heart or liver instead of earth worms.

Index of Scientific Names

Further Information

I. Other books by **Tetra Press:**

Beginners Aquarium Digest by Dr. U. Baensch / H. A. Baensch (1975)
Marine Care and Feeding Table by H. A. Baensch (1975)
Marine Aquarist's Manual by H. A. Baensch (1983)
Tropical Aquarium Fish by Dr. U. Baensch (1983)

II. Other useful books:

Aquariums by A. Evans (Feyles, 1976)
Fancy Goldfish Culture by F. W. Orme (Saiga, 1979)
Goldfish by J. Cobern (KR Books, 1978)
Ponds and Water Gardens by B. Heritage (Blandford, 1981)
Goldfish and Koi in Your Home by H. R. Axelrod / W. Vorderwinkler (T. F. H.)
Gardenponds by P. Stetson (T. F. H.)
Textbook of Fish Diseases by E. Amlacher (T. F. H., 1970)

III. Magazines

Aquarium Digest International, Tetra Sales (U.S.A.)
201, Tabor Road, Morris Plains, New Jersey, 07950. U.S.A.

or

c/o Tetra Information Centre
15, Newlay Lane Place, Leeds. LS13 2BB, Yorkshire. UK.

Tropical Fish Hobbyist Magazine, T. F. H. Publications Inc.
211, W. Sylvania Avenue, Neptune City, New Jersey, 07753. U.S.A.

or

c/o T. F. H. Publications Ltd.
11, Ormside Way, Holmethorpe Industrial Estate, Redhill RHI 2 PX. UK.

Aquarist and Pondkeeper
The Buckley Press, The Butts, Half Acre, Brentford, Middlesex. UK.

Practical Fishkeeping
EMAP National Publications, Bretton Court, Bretton, Peterborough. UK.

Freshwater and Marine Aquaria
120, West Sierra Madre Boulevard, Sierra Madre, California. 91024. U.S.A.

IV. Useful addresses

Federation of American Aquaria Societies
c/o Larry Brande
6601, S.W. 46th Street, Apt. 106., Davie, Florida. 33314. U.S.A.

Federation of British Aquatic Societies
c/o T. Butler
17, Risborough Road, Maidenhead, Berkshire, UK.

Photographs

Hans A. Baensch (4): 21, 24b, 29c, 32a
Peter Bauer (1): 31b
Gerhard Brünner (17): 26, 28, 29a, b, 30b–d, 31a, c, 32b–d, 33a–e
Hilmar Hansen (1): 38c
Burkard Kahl (3): 30a Pflanze, 34b, 37b
Dr. G. Kassebeer (2): 34c, 36d
Ryozo Komai (3): 44b, c, 45c
Shoichi Matsuda (1): 39d
Arend van den Nieuwenhuizen (11): Titelfoto, 34a, 35a–c, 36a, c, 38b, 39a, b, 41a
Aaron Norman (1): 39c
Klaus Paysan (15): 6, 15a, b, 17, 24a, c, d, 25a–d, 34d, 37a, 46b, 47a
N. Yoshimara (8): 67a–h
Rudolf Zukal (2): 30a Blüte im Kreisausschnitt, 38a
Tetra-Archiv:
Burkard Kahl (16): 9, 12, 41b, 42a–c, 43a, 44a, 45a, b, 46a, c, 47b, c, 54, 72
Gerhard Siepmann (1): 10
P. A. D. Sluyter (8): 18a–c, 19a–c, 20, 23

Illustrations

Monika Hänel, Angela Paysan and Tetra-Archiv

Further Information

I. Other books by **Tetra Press:**

Beginners Aquarium Digest by Dr. U. Baensch / H. A. Baensch (1975)
Marine Care and Feeding Table by H. A. Baensch (1975)
Marine Aquarist's Manual by H. A. Baensch (1983)
Tropical Aquarium Fish by Dr. U. Baensch (1983)

II. Other useful books:

Aquariums by A. Evans (Feyles, 1976)
Fancy Goldfish Culture by F. W. Orme (Saiga, 1979)
Goldfish by J. Cobern (KR Books, 1978)
Ponds and Water Gardens by B. Heritage (Blandford, 1981)
Goldfish and Koi in Your Home by H. R. Axelrod / W. Vorderwinkler (T. F. H.)
Gardenponds by P. Stetson (T. F. H.)
Textbook of Fish Diseases by E. Amlacher (T. F. H., 1970)

III. Magazines

Aquarium Digest International, Tetra Sales (U.S.A.)
201, Tabor Road, Morris Plains, New Jersey, 07950. U.S.A.

or

c/o Tetra Information Centre
15, Newlay Lane Place, Leeds. LS13 2BB, Yorkshire. UK.

Tropical Fish Hobbyist Magazine, T. F. H. Publications Inc.
211, W. Sylvania Avenue, Neptune City, New Jersey, 07753. U.S.A.

or

c/o T. F. H. Publications Ltd.
11, Ormside Way, Holmethorpe Industrial Estate, Redhill RHI 2 PX. UK.

Aquarist and Pondkeeper
The Buckley Press, The Butts, Half Acre, Brentford, Middlesex. UK.

Practical Fishkeeping
EMAP National Publications, Bretton Court, Bretton, Peterborough. UK.

Freshwater and Marine Aquaria
120, West Sierra Madre Boulevard, Sierra Madre, California. 91024. U.S.A.

IV. Useful addresses

Federation of American Aquaria Societies
c/o Larry Brande
6601, S.W. 46th Street, Apt. 106., Davie, Florida. 33314. U.S.A.

Federation of British Aquatic Societies
c/o T. Butler
17, Risborough Road, Maidenhead, Berkshire, UK.

Photographs

Illustrations